THE ANGUS GLENS

About the Author

Born in Edinburgh, James Carron has been based in Dundee for most of his life. With the Angus glens on his doorstep, he began walking there as a child and soon developed an enduring love for the area, exploring the hills and glens in all seasons and all weathers. In addition to day hikes, he also regularly embarks upon longer backpacking expeditions, camping out in wild and remote areas of the country.

While James spends much of his time in the Scottish hills, he makes regular forays overseas and has a particular passion for hiking in Eastern Europe.

A freelance writer specialising in active outdoor pursuits, he has written a number of walking guidebooks and is a regular contributor to the Wild Walks section of *TGO* magazine. He is also a regular contributor to *Scotland Outdoors* and BBC *Countryfile* magazines and has had articles published in a number of other publications including *Scotland Magazine*, *Scottish Memories*, *The Countryman* and *Camping*.

Visit www.walkscotland.net.

THE ANGUS GLENS

by James Carron

2 POLICE SQUARE, MILNTHORPE, CUMBRIA LA7 7PY
www.cicerone.co.uk

Printed in China on behalf of Latitude Press Ltd

A catalogue record for this book is available from the British Library.
All photographs are by the author unless otherwise stated.

Acknowledgements

I wish to thank David and Barbara Hogarth for route ideas and expert advice on the plants of the Angus glens and Angus Council's ranger service, Mountaineering Council of Scotland, Scottish Natural Heritage and Scottish Rights of Way and Access Society for a wealth of useful information without which the book would be incomplete. Thanks also go to various friends who accompanied me on forays into the glens over the years and individuals met along the way.

Advice to Readers

While every effort is made by our authors to ensure the accuracy of guidebooks as they go to print, changes can occur during the lifetime of an edition. If we know of any, there will be an Updates tab on this book's page on the Cicerone website (www.cicerone.co.uk), so please check before planning your trip. We also advise that you check information about such things as transport, accommodation and shops locally. Paths and tracks can be affected by forestry operations or work on the land, erosion, severe weather conditions or other factors. Even rights of way can be altered over time. We are always grateful for information about any discrepancies between a guidebook and the facts on the ground, sent by email to info@cicerone.co.uk or by post to Cicerone, 2 Police Square, Milnthorpe LA7 7PY, United Kingdom.

Front cover: River South Esk, Glen Clova and Hill of Strone (Walk 11)

CONTENTS

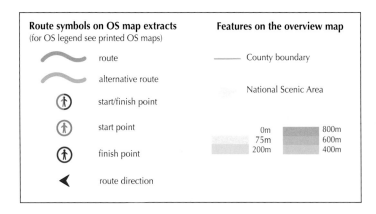

Route symbols on OS map extracts
(for OS legend see printed OS maps)

route

alternative route

start/finish point

start point

finish point

route direction

Features on the overview map

County boundary

National Scenic Area

0m	800m
75m	600m
200m	400m

Ladder Burn and the Mounth Road from Glenmark (Walk 30)

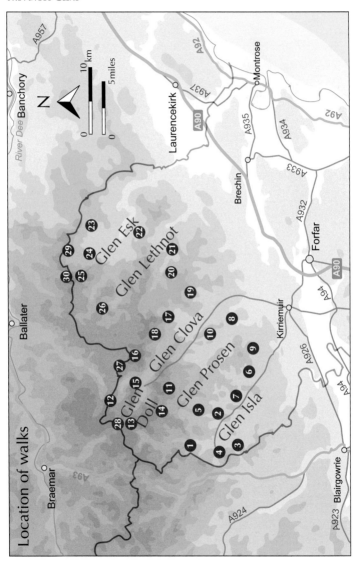

Location of walks

INTRODUCTION

A bird's-eye view over the glacial bowl of Corrie Fee and Glen Doll (Walk 14)

The five main glens of Angus – Isla, Prosen, Clova, Lethnot and Esk – radiate from the fertile plains of Strathmore deep into the southern ranges of the Cairngorms National Park. Each has its own distinct character and together they offer walkers exceptional variety.

Glen Clova is the most popular. From the car park at the end of the public road, Glen Doll and the valley of the River South Esk offer access to a clutch of Munros. Many walkers make a beeline for the contours above 3000 feet, but there are lots of less well-trod paths awaiting quiet exploration, ancient stalkers' paths and drove routes, like Jock's Road, the

Capel Mounth and Kilbo Path, providing ways through and over the hills.

Lurking below the high tops, U-shaped valleys with precipitous slopes soaring to airy ramparts of crags and cliffs and deep corrie lochans, such as Loch Brandy, offer physical evidence of the glacial power that carved out this landscape many millennia ago. The rocky amphitheatre of Corrie Fee, above Glen Doll, is one of the best examples of a moraine landscape in Scotland and is home to scarce alpine plants.

To the south of Clova, **Glen Prosen** is a sparsely populated valley, offering a less-frequented approach to the Munros of Driesh and Mayar

The Tolmounth rising over open ground above Glendoll Forest (Walk 28)

while, setting out from the landmark Airlie Monument, the line of low hills separating Prosen from Clova is one of the area's finest ridge walks.

Glen Isla is the most westerly of the Angus glens and is a land of contrasts. Following the River Isla upstream from the waterfalls at Reekie Linn, the terrain is initially relatively benign, gently undulating slopes carpeted in commercial forestry and rough pasture hiding artificial fishing lochs and reservoirs in fell-like folds. At its northern end the glen has a much wilder atmosphere as it tickles the craggy underbelly of Caenlochan Forest where hill tracks and stalkers' paths rise to the summits of Glas Maol and Creag Leacach.

Shorter glens radiate out from Isla's main spine: Glen Damff and Glen Finlet link with Prosen, while remote Canness Glen and Caenlochan Glen probe deep into the mountains.

Heading northeast, back over Prosen and Clova, **Glen Lethnot** is the least visited of the Angus glens. Wild and lonely, the valley offers a tempting choice of tracks and paths on to lower hills.

Completing the set, **Glen Esk** lies on the southern edge of the Grampian Mountains. It is a long, snaking valley, 15 miles of twisting tarmac ending just short of Invermark Lodge, a classic mid-Victorian shooting lodge overlooking Loch Lee. Sloping up from the road, an army of hills forms a frontier between Angus and Aberdeenshire. All worthy of ascent, they steadily gain in height until Mount Keen, the most easterly of Scotland's Munros, is

Water of Mark flowing through Glen Mark; conservation work has been undertaken here to encourage spawning salmon (Walk 25)

reached. Below the tops, a network of ancient byways is now the preserve of walkers and backpackers.

As diverse as they are, with their own unique characteristics, the Angus glens combine to offer the walker a rich blend of landscape, geology and natural habitat, encompassing high mountain peaks and lower hills, glacial valleys, corries and moraine, natural and managed forestry, lochs and man-made reservoirs, cascading upland burns and gently meandering rivers. Not only is the scenery exceptionally varied and the views nothing short of awe-inspiring, but there is also a great profusion of plants, birds and wildlife.

While they may feel rugged and remote, all five glens are remarkably accessible and, thanks to the A90, are within easy reach of Dundee. Despite this, they remain a relatively peaceful and crowd-free escape for walkers. The routes offer a selection of moderate to challenging hill and mountain walks suitable for capable hillwalkers.

LANDSCAPE

The Angus glens are a product of the Ice Age, glaciers the architects of both upland and lowland terrain. In their wake, these snaking rivers of ice left behind well-sculpted peaks, deep U-shaped valleys and cavernous armchair-like corries.

While the upper reaches of the glens – cloaked in crags and cliffs – remain hostile and rugged, the

gathering of sediment over thousands of years created fertile plains lower down the valleys. These were settled by early farmers. While Neolithic sites and several Iron Age earth houses have been found, most of the archaeological remains uncovered date from medieval or later times. Early evidence of farming includes turf dykes and the ruins of shielings (small stone-built cottages located on higher pasture). Rig and furrow, a traditional system of cultivating land practised until the mid-19th century, is evident across the area.

In the 1850s, in common with much of the Scottish Highlands, families were cleared from the land to make way for large sheep farms and the population fell sharply. The glens continue to support agriculture and communities, albeit on a much smaller scale than once was the case.

Between this flat land and the mountain peaks and plateaus above, the moors may at first glance appear wild and untamed but this belies the heavy influence of man. Vast areas of land are managed for sport – grouse and pheasant shooting, deer stalking and fishing the main activities. Alongside farming this is the mainstay of the local economy. Heather burning, vermin control, the construction of hill tracks and the retention of remote cottages and lodges are just a few of the ways these sporting activities impact on the lie of the land.

Where ground has been deemed unviable for either farming or sport, commercial forestry has taken root. Glen Clova (including Glen Doll), Glen Isla and Glen Prosen all have extensive plantations while, over recent years, concerted efforts have been made to restore native woodlands.

WILDLIFE

The Angus glens are home to an array of wildlife. However, some species are much more likely to be spotted by walkers than others. In the hills and valleys, **red** and **roe deer** are common. While reds tend to roam the hills and glens in sizeable herds, roes are more solitary creatures, often spotted on the fringes of woodland or lurking in undergrowth. Occasionally they will stray onto open ground or flit over roads.

On the high ground **mountain hare** are a frequent sight while rabbits are endemic, often sharing rough pasture with sheep, cattle and opportunistic carrion crows. Rabbits offer rich pickings for stoats and foxes. Unlike rabbit and brown hare, mountain hare are indigenous to Scotland.

Sheep – one of the main sources of income for Angus farmers – are found on low and high ground while cattle – including the distinctive shaggy Highland cow – tend to occupy fields down in the valleys.

Forests offer a safe haven for the increasingly threatened **red squirrel**. Thanks to its relative isolation, Glen Doll has a stable population of around 100 and colonies also exist in the other glens where grey squirrels – the biggest threat to the reds – have yet to gain a foothold.

An iconic Highland cow resting by Buckhood Cottage, Glen Prosen

The woodlands of Glen Doll in particular are home to the **pine marten** which, although rare, has benefited in recent years from measures to conserve its habitat. A cat-sized member of the weasel family, the pine marten thrives in rocky woodland terrain and is most often sighted at dawn or dusk. It is, however, very wary of humans and will disappear in an instant.

The field vole, wood mouse and hedgehog are among smaller mammals that may be seen on lower ground while otter, bank vole and water vole live around rivers, streams and lochs. Healthy populations of **otter** have been recorded along the length of the River South Esk. **Water vole** numbers, however, are less stable. Once plentiful, this native species has been decimated by invading American mink, first imported into Britain in the 1920s and farmed for fur. However, conservation work, particularly in Corrie Fee, has seen some recovery in water vole numbers while mink trapping – designed to protect ground-nesting birds and their eggs – is an integral part of land management.

The most elusive creature in the Angus glens is the **Scottish wildcat**. Using concealed camera traps, the Cairngorms Wildcat Project has confirmed sightings in Glen Clova while reports suggest small populations in the other Angus glens.

The only venomous snake walkers may encounter is the **adder**.

Relatively common on heather moor and around the fringes of woodland, they are most frequently spotted in hot weather sunning themselves on rocks or lying across paths. The adder has a distinctive dark zigzag running down the length of the spine and an inverted 'V' shape on the neck. Males are generally white or pale grey with a black zigzag while females are a pale brown colour, with a darker brown zigzag. Adders are not aggressive, but if bitten by one seek medical assistance as soon as possible.

Atlantic salmon and sea trout migrate up the rivers of Angus. The River North Esk and River South Esk are both popular with anglers, while inland lochs and reservoirs are renowned for their brown trout.

Birds

Red grouse are bred for sport throughout the glens and will pop up out of the heather when least expected while another game bird, the pheasant, is most likely to be spotted in fields, woodland, or dodging traffic on the roads. On rocky summits and slopes, **ptarmigan** are more elusive. In winter they are completely white, while in summer only the wings remain white. The best time to spot them is early spring, before their winter plumage is lost.

Golden eagle, peregrine falcon and raven all breed on crags and may be seen soaring above cliffs and rocky slopes. Corrie Fee, Glen Doll and the valley of the River South Esk below Bachnagairn are particularly good spots for sightings. The buzzard is the most prevalent bird of prey in the glens and may be seen flying over both low and high ground.

At the other end of the spectrum, the **white-tailed eagle** (also known as the sea eagle) is an occasional visitor thanks to an ongoing reintroduction project at Tentsmuir Forest, Fife, 40km to the south. The **osprey**, which returns annually to nesting sites in the neighbouring county of Perthshire, has been recorded fishing lochs and reservoirs in Angus.

Coniferous plantations are home to the **great spotted woodpecker** (more frequently heard rather than seen), plus the common crossbill and the smallest of all European birds, the

goldcrest. Woodlands are also good places to spot the willow warbler, cuckoo, jay, jackdaw, siskin, chaffinch and various tits, including the coal tit, great tit and blue tit.

On rough pasture and heathland oystercatcher and curlew are common, while Angus is a breeding stronghold for the **ring ouzel**, similar in size to a blackbird but with a distinctive white chest ring and longer wings and tail.

PLANTS AND FLOWERS

While the ancient glens were once heavily wooded, the hand of man has seen intervention both detrimental and beneficial to the natural landscape over the centuries.

Scots pine trees in Glen Lee (Walk 26)

15

Our Neolithic ancestors cut much of the original timber down, creating arable fields and grassy pasture in lowland areas while much of the higher ground ended up as open moor. Trees returned in the form of sizeable commercial plantations while in more recent times there has been a concerted effort to both plant and encourage the natural regeneration of native species such as rowan, beech, birch and ash, a step towards redressing the balance. Airy woodlands of **Scots pine** and larch provide a welcome breather from more densely packed forests of spruce and lodgepole pine.

Large tracts of moor are managed for shooting, resulting in a patchwork of heather and grass. Grazing by sheep, cattle and deer restrict plant diversity here. Tussocks of hare's-tail cotton grass grow in all but the wettest areas, while cross-leaved heath and crowberry are widespread. Gorse and broom add a splash of yellow during the summer while bracken provides valuable cover for birds and small animals. Rocks and boulders support various lichens, and the iconic Scottish thistle is a common sight.

Purple and white foxgloves grow in the valleys, bluebells and yellow primroses carpet many of the native woodlands and meadows of wild flowers are to be found on less intensely grazed slopes.

A foxglove adds colour to Glendoll Forest (Walk 14)

Slender yet resilient harebells survive the harshest conditions in Corrie Fee (Walk 14)

The region's rarest plants are to be found on high ground where some of the most ancient species survive in the testing environment. Corrie Fee, above Glen Doll, is noted for its **purple coltsfoot** and **yellow oxytropis** and is also home to more common mountain plants: purple saxifrage, yellow mountain saxifrage, roseroot and globeflower. Neighbouring Corrie Shalloch has the largest area of **mountain willow scrub** in Britain.

Above the corries, on the vast windswept Caenlochan plateau, a remarkably diverse range of habitats exists, incorporating dwarf-shrub and heath, mire, grassland and an array of **alpine grasses**, **lichens** and **flowers**. The area is regarded as one of the best upland botanical sites in the country.

WEATHER

The Angus glens offer year-round walking, although the best conditions are usually to be found between May and September when the weather is generally drier and temperatures are, on the whole, higher. Although rainfall is typically lower than in the west of Scotland, prolonged wet spells and fleeting heavy showers, even on sunny days, are becoming an increasingly common part of the summer weather pattern.

Despite the relatively compact geographical nature of the Angus glens, the weather can vary across the area and it is often possible to find good conditions in one glen when the weather is less favourable in others. As a result there is plenty of scope for choosing routes that take advantage of this local variation.

It is worth paying particular attention to cloud base. While the higher ground may be shrouded in heavy cloud or blanketed in mist, lower hills may dip below the ceiling, offering alternative days out. Always be prepared for descending cloud or mist and be equipped to navigate in bad visibility, particularly across featureless terrain where map, compass and the ability to use them come into their own.

Prolonged spells of wet weather do have an impact on hill paths and tracks, particularly those crossing peaty or marshy ground, making the terrain more difficult to negotiate.

Over the mountains, snow can fall at any time of the year. In reality, however, snow can usually be expected between November and March, although it can linger in the high corries well into the spring. During the winter, blizzards are common across exposed high plateaux and mountain peaks. While avalanche risk is low, heavy snow can render high-level routes impassable. Walks 1, 12–16, 25 and, 27–30 are those most likely to be affected by adverse weather conditions.

Depending on the severity of conditions, heavy and drifting snowfall can block access roads while icy conditions can make driving conditions in the glens hazardous.

HERITAGE PATHS AND HISTORY

The Angus glens are criss-crossed by a network of old rights of way, long-established tracks and paths that run through the valleys and over the hills. Once vital links used by drovers, shepherds, traders and even smugglers, most fell by the wayside, superseded by modern highways. Now they are the preserve of walkers, backpackers and mountain bikers.

One of the most famous is the **Tolmounth** (Walk 30), a high-level route linking Glen Clova with Braemar. Better known as Jock's Road, it played a key role in Scottish rights of way history. In 1887 a group of shepherds who regularly used the road joined forces with the Scottish Rights of Way Society to challenge a landowner who was intent on denying them access. After a lengthy legal battle that ended in the House of Lords in 1888, the old road was established as a right of way, setting a precedent that has protected public access to scores of other routes in the Scottish hills.

Negotiating high, exposed and largely featureless terrain, the Tolmounth is a challenging journey, particularly during the winter when the high ground is frequently swept by storms or blanketed in snow. It is among a number of old routes known as the Mounth Roads, so called because the range of hills between Angus and Deeside was historically known as the Mounth. Two – the Cairnwell and Cairn o'Mount – were

incorporated into the road network while others, like the **Capel Mounth** (Walk 27), **Mounth** (Walk 28) and **Firmounth** (Walk 29) gradually fell out of use but remain an integral part of the landscape.

The Mounth Roads and a network of stalkers' paths and hill tracks are a great resource for walkers, providing access to the high ground or offering satisfying day or multi-day hikes in their own right.

The only official long-distance path to meander into Angus is the **Cateran Trail**, a 103km (64-mile) circular route that, for the majority of users,

A carved Cateran Trail waymarker depicts the weathered features of a cattle rustler (Walk 2)

begins and ends in Blairgowrie, in the neighbouring county of Perthshire. Heading north through the Perthshire countryside to Spittal of Glenshee via Bridge of Cally, Kirkmichael and Enochdu, the route turns south, crossing into Angus below Mount Blair. Passing through the hamlet of Forter, the way continues south through Glen Isla, passing Auchintaple Loch and Loch Shandra en route to Kirkton of Glenisla. From there, it heads south to Bridge of Craigisla beyond which it leaves Angus.

The trail is named after marauding cattle rustlers known at Caterans, who terrorised farmers from the Middle Ages until the 17th century and made good use of old drove roads and hill tracks to flee with stolen livestock. A quirky feature of the route is the carved wooden waymarker posts that feature bearded Cateran faces.

DECIPHERING PLACE NAMES

While some of the earliest place names in Angus derive from Pictish words, many of the mountain and hill names commonly in use today have Gaelic or Scots roots. One Pictish term 'monadh', meaning 'mountain range', was adopted by the Gaels to describe an upland moor or hill and the word is present in other forms, including 'mounth' and the Anglicised 'mount'. Mount Keen comes from the Gaelic name 'Monadh Caoin', meaning 'gentle hill' while Mount Blair translates as 'hill of the plain' and Tolmount as 'hill of the valley'. The Firmounth, Am Monadh Giuthais in Gaelic, means 'the moor of pine'.

The Gaelic word 'creag' ('craig' in Scots), describes a crag or mountain, and makes frequent appearances on the county's maps. Creag Leacach, for example, is the 'slabby crag', an apt description given its rock-strewn slopes. The word 'carn' ('cairn' in Scots) indicates a cairn-shaped hill or mountain and inspired names such as Cairn Bannoch, 'the peaked hill'. Other hills in the county with Gaelic names include Tom Buidhe (yellow hill), Glas Maol (grey or pale hill) and Mayar, thought to derive from 'magh ard', meaning 'high plain'.

Another word walkers will often encounter is 'corrie'. It comes from the Gaelic term 'coire' and is used to describe a rounded hollow in a hillside. Corrie Fee, for example, means 'corrie of the deer'.

As Gaelic gradually gave way to Scots in the glens, new words appeared, such as 'shank', meaning a long ridge (rising from Glen Lee, the Shank of Inchgrundle is a fine example), and 'burn', a term used frequently in Scotland to describe a stream.

HILL TABLES

A number of the mountains and hills in this guide are classified as Munros, Corbetts or Grahams.

Crossing open ground en route to the distinctive cone of Broad Cairn (Walk 12)

- Munros are separate Scottish mountains over 3000ft (914.4m) in height. The original list was drawn up by Sir Hugh Munro and published in 1891. It is subject to occasional revision, and currently (SMC, 2012) stands at 282.
- Corbetts are Scottish peaks over 2500ft (762m) in height but under 3000ft (914.4m) with a reascent of 500ft (152.4m) on all sides (220 peaks are listed at present). Mr J Rooke Corbett compiled the original list in the 1920s.
- Grahams are a more recent offering, a complete list of Scottish hills between 2000ft (610m) and 2499ft (761m) in height with a drop of at least 150m (492ft) on all sides. The table was compiled by Alan Dawson and Fiona Torbet (née Graham), and includes 224 hills.

The summits covered in this guide include 9 Munros, 3 Corbetts and 7 Grahams.

PLANNING AND PREPARATION

Walking in Scotland is generally a safe activity, although – as with all outdoor pursuits – there is a level of inherent risk. Good preparation and planning play a key role in minimising the chances of getting into difficulties.

Before setting out consider whether fitness levels, experience, available equipment and hill skills of every member of the party meet the demands of the walk. Avoid taking unnecessary risks by tackling an overly long or difficult route. Do not hesitate to cut a walk short if someone tires or if the terrain becomes too difficult. It is better to retreat with all limbs intact rather than push on and risk accident, injury or illness.

It is a good idea to leave word of the intended walk with a responsible friend, relative or neighbour before setting off from home. If on holiday, details may be left with a hostel warden, B&B owner or hotel manager. It is important that contact is made with the person upon return to let them know you are back safely. If you fail to return at a predetermined time the relevant authorities can be alerted and, if necessary, a search or rescue mounted.

A route card – recording name and contact details, a note of everyone in the party, parking location, vehicle registration number, mobile phone number, start date, time and grid reference, intended route and end date, time and grid reference – is an efficient way of leaving details. In Glen Doll, the ranger service provides route cards that can be completed and left at the ranger centre adjacent to the main public car park. Don't forget to collect your route card when you return so as to prevent an unnecessary rescue callout.

Always check the weather forecast before setting out. Television channels, radio stations and newspapers all offer outlooks, while more detailed local forecasts can be found online or at tourist information centres and outdoor and countryside centres. Tailor activities to the weather and be prepared to cut a walk short if conditions deteriorate. The Scottish weather is remarkably unpredictable and it is not uncommon to experience a wide variety of conditions in a single day. However well equipped and prepared a walker is, persistent rain and relentless wind can quickly deplete reserves of energy and erode morale.

Glendoll Forest and a cloudy Driesh from the Capel Mounth (Walk 27)

While bad weather can spoil a good walk, hot and sunny conditions can be equally unsettling. More liquid must be carried and consumed, while sunburn and heat stroke present very real dangers to the unwary.

ESSENTIAL EQUIPMENT

Clothing

Proper footwear is vital, and due to the varied nature of the terrain hillwalking boots are recommended. A good pair of waterproof **boots** with soles that offer a high level of grip will keep feet dry, warm and comfortable. Ensure new boots are broken in properly to remove stiffness and reduce the risk of blisters before embarking upon longer walks. Those planning to explore the higher peaks in winter should consider four-season or mountaineering boots

Boots should be coupled with good-quality walking **socks**; the best ones have extra padding around the toe and heel areas. Many walkers prefer to wear two pairs of socks – a thin pair next to the skin with a thicker pair on top – to prevent blisters. Make sure the thin pair does not have raised seams, and avoid socks that are too large or too small, heavily worn or full of holes.

Gaiters will come in handy where routes cross rough heather moor, grassland and reedy patches of ground.

Dressing successfully for the hills is best achieved through a layering system. Clothing can be easily added or removed depending on the weather, temperature or level of activity. A selection of thin layers traps more warm air than a single thick jersey or fleece.

The **base layer** (closest to the skin) can be a thin T-shirt, vest or thermal underwear top. Avoid natural fabrics like cotton – which trap and hold sweat – and go for a quick-drying synthetic fibre capable of transferring perspiration away from the skin. Fleeces are ideal **mid-layers**, as are sweatshirts and jumpers. The third and final **outer layer**, or shell, should be waterproof, windproof and, ideally, breathable. It is always a good idea to pack an extra layer or two, particularly when venturing on to higher ground where temperatures tend to be much lower, and can be reduced considerably by wind chill.

Trousers should be lightweight, loose fitting and preferably quick drying. **Shorts** are excellent for summer walking, but pack long trousers as a route may cross areas of brambles, nettles or thistles. Carry waterproof trousers too.

Take a **warm hat** and **gloves** throughout the year, and in summer pack a **wide-brimmed hat** to protect head and neck from the sun.

Food and drink

Taking sufficient food and liquid are essential. Hillwalking burns calories at a higher rate than normal activity and these must be replenished throughout the day. Prior to setting off, meals high in carbohydrates – such as rice and pasta – offer long-term slow-release energy. While on the hill, eating little and often is a good philosophy. Sandwiches and snack foods (for example sausage rolls and pork pies) are convenient and filling while dried fruit, seeds and nuts, and cereal bars, provide natural sugars and protein. High-sugar products (chocolate bars and sweets) offer rapid bursts of energy.

Fluid must also be replaced on a regular basis, and drinking little and often is a better way to avoid dehydration than waiting until thirsty before taking a drink. Carry plenty of liquid, particularly on hotter days when consumption will be significantly higher. As an estimate 1.5 litres should be sufficient for a day walk.

Supplementing supplies by collecting water in the hills is a matter of personal choice. While standing water and low-level streams and rivers – particularly those in agricultural areas – should be avoided, fast-flowing streams on high ground are less likely to be contaminated. There is, however, no guarantee that the water can be safely consumed unless treated with water purification tablets or a water purifier.

What to take
To carry the gear necessary for a day in the hills, a rucksack with a 30-litre capacity should suffice. Items that need to stay dry, such as spare

clothing, mobile phone and camera equipment, should be kept in a waterproof liner within the sack.

The following is a list of essential items that should be carried on any of the walks in this guidebook.
• waterproof jacket
• waterproof trousers
• spare fleece
• hat
• gloves
• food and liquid
• map(s)
• compass
• whistle
• torch
• first aid kit
• survival bag
• mobile phone
• pencil and paper.

In summer, add a sun hat and sun cream to the list. Pack insect repellent too. Midges are becoming increasingly prevalent in Angus between May and September and are most commonly encountered during periods of calm warm weather. Lowland moor, grassland and woodland are all potential hot spots for these airborne irritants. A midge forecast for Scotland can be found online (www.midgeforecast.co.uk).

FIRST AID

Walkers should have a basic knowledge of first aid and carry a small first aid kit, available from outdoor shops and pharmacies, including the following items:

- waterproof, breathable plasters of various sizes
- sterile dressings
- triangular bandage
- eye pad
- crêpe bandage
- safety pins (to secure dressings)
- pair of disposable latex gloves
- antiseptic cream or wipes
- small pair of scissors.
  Other useful items include:
- personal medication
- painkillers
- antihistamine cream
- pair of tweezers
- cigarette lighter or matches
- insect repellent.

The best way to learn the basics of first aid is to take a course: a GP surgery or pharmacy is a good first point of contact. There are many private providers, as well as larger organisations such as the St John Ambulance Association (www.sja.org.uk) and, in Scotland, the St Andrew's Ambulance Association (www.firstaid.org.uk). A useful pocket guide *First Aid and Wilderness Medicine* by Drs Jim Duff and Peter Gormly is published by Cicerone.

Three other items of kit will come in useful in the event of an emergency. One of the most important is a survival bag, which will protect a casualty from wind, rain and cold. Keep one at the bottom of the rucksack at all times. Every walker should also carry a whistle and torch for attracting attention. Note that in the Angus glens mobile phone reception ranges from poor to non-existent over much of the low ground, although signal strength is much better on high ground and summits.

Thankfully accidents in the countryside are rare, and the majority are

Water of Saughs and the brooding crags of Corrie Berran from Tamhilt (Walk 21)

relatively minor. Blisters, probably the most common affliction among hill-walkers, should be dressed to avoid further rubbing. Relieve sprains and twists by binding tightly with a crêpe bandage to enable the casualty to return, albeit slowly, to civilisation where the injury can be properly treated.

More testing (and thankfully infrequent) conditions such as hypothermia and heat exhaustion are best combatted through good preparation and early recognition. Wearing adequate warm clothing and avoiding long stops in cold weather will prevent hypothermia. Early signs include tiredness, listlessness and irritability. Heat exhaustion can be avoided by regularly taking on fluids. Early symptoms include tiredness, light-headedness and muscle cramps. Rest up in a shady place, drink plenty and, if possible, eat sweet and salty foods.

In the event of serious injury or illness the rescue services may need to be contacted, although making such a call is not a matter to be treated lightly.

The casualty must be made as comfortable as possible, and the injuries assessed. If he cannot be moved, expert help will have to be called. The rescue services will need as much information as possible so make a written note of the casualty's name, age and the type of injuries; details on the cause of the accident and the time it occurred; the terrain and any potential hazards (prevailing weather conditions, avalanche, rock fall and so on). Record the grid reference and details of the availability of torches, mobile phones, group shelters and medical personnel at the scene.

If there is a mobile phone signal dial 999, ask for police, and explain the situation clearly and concisely. If there is no signal, try climbing to a higher point where one may be found. If this fails, send the most able person in the group for help. If this is not possible – or if you are the casualty and alone – signal for help with a whistle and/or torch.

The International Distress Signal consists of six blasts of the whistle (or flashes of the torch), followed by a minute's silence, then another six blasts. This drill is repeated every minute. The response is three whistle blasts, followed by a minute's silence, then another three blasts. Continue giving the signal at regular intervals until help arrives. Make the location of the casualty site as prominent as possible: use brightly coloured clothes and kit, light a fire and make as much noise as possible.

Await rescue and never give up hope. One of the most vital aspects of first aid in such a situation is to maintain individual and/or group morale.

GETTING THERE AND WHERE TO STAY

The Angus glens are all accessed by road from the south. For Isla, Prosen and Clova, Kirriemuir, six miles west of the county town of Forfar, is the main gateway. Leave the A90 at Kirriemuir

A wealth of landscape and wildlife information can be found at Glen Doll Ranger Base (Walks 12–16, 27 and 28)

Junction, just north of Forfar. Isla can also be approached from Alyth in Perthshire, to the south, or from Glen Shee, to the west. Lethnot and Esk are accessed from Brechin, also on the A90, via Edzell. The glens are all well signed from the A90.

While accommodation and other services are limited in the glens themselves, a good selection of places to stay and eat and a full range of services can be found in Forfar, Kirriemuir and Brechin. There are campsites in Forfar and Brechin and near Kirriemuir. The nearest city is Dundee, to the south.

Isla has one hotel, at Kirkton of Glenisla (www.glenisla-hotel.com). Accommodation can also be found to the north, outwith the glen, at Spittal of Glenshee where there are two hotels (www.spittalofglenshee.

co.uk and www.dalmunzie.com) and a bunkhouse (www.gulabinoutdoors. co.uk). There is a guesthouse at Glenmarkie (www.glenmarkie.co.uk) and various self-catering lets in the glen. There are no shops or campsites in Isla. Public toilets are located at the Backwater Dam.

Prosen has a bunkhouse (www. prosenhostel.co.uk) in Glenprosen Village and there are various self-catering lets in the glen. There are no shops, campsites or public toilets in Prosen.

Glen Clova has a hotel and bunkhouse (www.clovahotel.com) in the hamlet of Clova. While older maps show a youth hostel and campsite near Acharn in Glen Doll, both have been closed for a number of years. There are three designated short-stay wild camping sites in Glen Doll – one on Jock's Road (NO 252 766), one in a former quarry above Acharn (NO 280 764) and one by the River South Esk to the south of Moulzie (NO 285 768). Elsewhere in the glen, there is a scattering of self-catering cottages. There are no shops or formal campsites in Clova. Public toilets can be found in the car park at Milton of Clova and at Glen Doll Ranger Base.

Lethnot has no accommodation or services.

Esk has a formal campsite (www.gleneskcaravanpark.co.uk) at the southern end of the glen and an informal camping field at Tarfside with public toilets in the adjacent car park. There are a number of self-catering holiday cottages in the glen and refreshments can be found during the summer season at The Retreat, near Tarfside (www.glenesk.dreamhosters.com).

As there are no fuel stations in the glens, motorists should ensure tanks are filled in one of the main towns before setting off.

See Appendix B for more information to help you plan your trip.

PUBLIC TRANSPORT

The main gateways to the glens – Forfar, Kirriemuir and Brechin – are well served by buses. Stagecoach Strathtay (www.stagecoachbus.com) operates local services and there are regular links to Dundee, while Scottish Citylink's Dundee to Aberdeen coach service (www.citylink.co.uk) stops in Forfar.

By contrast, the glens themselves are not easily accessed by public transport (www.angus.gov.uk/transport). Careful planning is required along with an acceptance that a good number of

The Goal from Craigs of Lethnot on the elevated Airlie Ridge (Walk 8)

the routes in this guidebook are currently outwith the scope of the bus network. What services there are tend to revolve around school runs – term-time only – and Demand Responsive Services where travellers request a timetabled journey in advance otherwise it will not operate.

With this in mind, it is possible to travel from Kirriemuir to Clova and Braedowie, in Glen Doll; from Kirriemuir to Dykehead, at the junction of Clova and Prosen; from Brechin to Invermark in Glen Esk; from Brechin to Tillybardine, in Glen Lethnot; and from Kirriemuir or Blairgowrie to Kirkton of Glenisla and on to Auchavan in Glen Isla.

Rail services (www.scotrail.co.uk) in Angus are confined to the coast and

walkers arriving in the county by train are advised to alight in Dundee for the best selection of onward bus services or car rental opportunities. Dundee also has an airport (www.hial.co.uk/dundee-airport) with flights to and from London City.

See Appendix B for further information.

ACCESS: RIGHTS AND RESPONSIBILITIES

Walkers in Scotland have long enjoyed the right to roam on just about any land, with no requirements to stay on defined paths or rights of way. This position was ratified with the implementation of the Land Reform (Scotland) Act 2003 which

A perfect pitch – wild camping by the Firmounth above Glen Esk (Walk 29)

gives everyone the right to be on most land provided they act responsibly. To help people enjoy Scotland's outdoors responsibly, the Scottish Outdoor Access Code was drawn up as part of the bill. The main points of the code relevant to hillwalkers are summarised below.

- Take responsibility for your own actions.
- Respect people's privacy and peace of mind.
- Help land managers and others to work safely and effectively.
- Care for your environment.
- Keep your dog under proper control.

The freedom to roam does have some restrictions. In common with many rural parts of Scotland, Angus has a good many sporting estates where animals and birds such as red deer and grouse are shot, whether for sport or conservation. These estates derive a significant amount of their income from shooting and it is an important part of the rural economy.

Deer management takes place at various times of the year but the most sensitive period is the stag-stalking season which runs from 1 July to 20 October. The grouse-shooting season runs from 12 August to 10 December. Most of this activity takes place on open hillside and tends to be away from popular walking routes. That said, a number of routes in the guide do cross land where both deer stalking and grouse shooting take place.

During the shooting seasons it is recommended that walkers do their best to seek permission from the relevant landowner before setting off. Generally the estates in Angus try to be as accommodating as possible and will often give useful advice on areas to avoid or alternative routes. As part of the Scottish Outdoor Access Code, Scottish Natural Heritage operates an online service called Heading for the Scottish Hills (www.outdooraccess-scotland.com/hftsh) that provides deer-stalking information for various estates, including a number in Angus (see Appendix B for further contact details). Stalking and shooting do not generally take place on a Sunday.

During the shooting seasons, walkers can assist landowners by heeding the following points.

- Follow reasonable advice given including Heading for the Scottish Hills messages, deer management group leaflets, notices at parking places or by estate staff encountered.
- Take reasonable steps to find out where stalking and shooting is taking place and take account of advice on alternative routes.
- Use paths where available.
- Consult estates about plans if organising a large group walk.
- Avoid wild camping in corries.
- Keep voices to reasonable levels as sound carries in the hills.
- Keep dogs on a short lead or under close control.

- Avoid cutting down through corries, and if this is not possible follow the main watercourse through the corrie.
- Follow mountain ridges where possible.

The following are also useful tips for responsible walking.

- Minimise disturbance to livestock, especially during the lambing season (March–May). Dogs should be kept on a short lead at all times near sheep and cows. Never let a dog worry or attack sheep or cattle and be particularly careful when crossing ground where cows are accompanied by their calves. Cows are very protective of their young and there have been incidents when walkers with dogs have

been seriously injured or killed by stampeding cattle, panicked by the sight of dogs. If this happens to you, it is better to let your dog off its lead as it will make its own escape without endangering you.

- On open hillsides, moor and grassland, dogs should be kept on a short lead or under close control during the bird-nesting season (April–July). If a dog is prone to give chase, keep it under close control in areas where there may be wild animals like rabbits, hare and deer or birds such as pheasants and grouse.
- Do not disturb wildlife or damage the environment by interfering with the habitats of birds and animals or picking plants or flowers.

Pausing for a rest by the Tolmouth with superb views over Glen Doll (Walk 28)

Glen Lethnot

- Stick to paths and tracks where possible to avoid damaging ground vegetation and keep to the centre of the path to avoid further widening it or creating additional erosion. Avoid damaging walls and fences by climbing over them and wherever possible use stiles or gates. If a fence has to be crossed, do so at a post to avoid straining wires. Leave gates as you find them.

- From time to time temporary access restrictions may be encountered. This could, for example, be a forest track closed due to tree felling, or a path shut because of bad erosion. Usually a diversion will be offered; if there is no diversion, consult the map and work out an alternative or curtail the route.

USING THIS GUIDE

The walks are divided into six sections, one for each of the main Angus glens and the sixth offering a selection of hill-path routes following established rights of way. While the majority of the walks are circular, the hill paths are linear routes offering scope for longer, multi-day treks.

The route descriptions all begin with an information box noting the start point for each walk, including a brief description and grid reference, plus advice on the availability of car parking. The distance, height gain and time required to complete the route is also listed. The time quoted is an estimate based on Naismith's Rule and does not include rest or meal breaks.

Details of maps required to safely navigate the route are also given.

Glen Isla

The maps published in the guide are from the Ordnance Survey 1:50,000 Landranger series. It is strongly recommended that rather than relying solely on these map extracts walkers carry the relevant OS 1:50,000 Landranger or OS 1:25,000 Explorer sheet (the latter offers a much greater level of detail). Gaelic spellings used in the route descriptions all follow those used on the Ordnance Survey maps for ease of correlation.

A summary of the route follows, offering a brief overview of what can be expected in terms of terrain and the level of walking and navigational experience required. The guide assumes a basic level of hillwalking experience, the knowledge to read and understand maps and relate this information to the physical landscape and the ability to navigate competently using map and compass.

The majority of the routes follow established tracks and paths while features such as fence lines, walls, streams and forestry assist with route-finding. However, on some routes, sections cross open ground where there are few easily identifiable physical landmarks and where paths are either indistinct or non-existent. It is in such circumstances that the ability to navigate is essential.

GLEN ISLA

A view of Badandun Hill from woodland above Craighead (Walk 2)

WALK 1

Monega Hill, Glas Maol, Creag Leacach and Monamenach

Start/Finish	Auchavan, 10km north of Kirkton of Glenisla (NO 192 698)
Distance	21km (13 miles)
Time	7hr
Height gain	1242m (4075ft)
Maps	OS 1:50,000 Landranger 43; OS 1:25,000 Explorer 387

For two mountains in such close proximity, Glas Maol and Creag Leacach could not contrast more. The summit of the former is an unremarkable dome while the latter's angular backbone rips sharply through the skyline, showering a cascade of rock and scree down either side.

This is a long, demanding walk combining the two Munros with ascents of outlying Monega Hill, at the start of the route, and Monamenach, at the end. The walk initially follows the Monega Path, a right of way and former trade route between the glen and Braemar. A high, exposed and featureless plateau is crossed so accurate route-finding, particularly in poor visibility, is a must. That said, good tracks and paths exist for the majority of the walk and the terrain is generally excellent. Dogs should be kept under close control due to the presence of grazing sheep and ground-nesting birds.

Where the public road through Glen Isla ends at **Auchavan** (parking area), an estate track continues north to Tulchan Lodge and beyond. This enables swift progress to be made, the route following the River Isla upstream into an increasingly wild and lonely glen.

The walking is easy and at **Tulchan Lodge**, a remote and very private shooting lodge shrouded in woodland, remain on the track, ignoring a bridge spanning the river. The track continues north, skirting the eastern edge of forestry, to reach a sturdy green metal Scottish Rights of Way and Access Society sign for 'The Monega Path to Braemar'.

It is tempting to strike out over the hillside from this point, following the line the sign suggests. However, to avoid a lumpy tramp over rough heather and across a stream gully, stay on the track a little longer, crossing the **Glas Burn**. Once over, bear left on a distinct path and the ascent of **Monega Hill** begins in earnest.

The climb is initially steep, but the gradient becomes more manageable as the path swings north, passing through a collapsed gate before taking a well-graded line up the long spine. As height is gained, pause occasionally to catch breath and enjoy excellent views south over Glen Isla and east to the mountains above Glen Doll.

Although the right of way bypasses the summit, a well-walked path, dotted with small cairns, leads straight to it. Here the hill ends abruptly, rough slopes plunging steeply into Caenlochan Glen below. Rarely visited, this lost valley of cliffs, crags and glacial moraine is prized for its mountain flora and alpine grasses. ▸

On a clear day, the bird's-eye view over the glen from Monega Hill is breathtaking.

Rejoin the Monega Path in the shallow col to the west of the summit and the way ambles over **Little Glas Maol** towards Glas Maol. It is not unusual to spot large herds of red deer roaming across the plateau here. Look out too for mountain hare.

THE MONEGA ROAD

The Monega Road is the highest of the Mounth Roads linking Angus and Aberdeenshire. Unlike many of Scotland's ancient highways and byways, it crosses a mountain plateau rather than passing through a valley, making it a serious and potentially dangerous proposition for early travellers, particularly during the winter when heavy snow could obliterate the route from the landscape. Historical evidence indicates there was a hospital at the northern end, probably frequently used by casualties of the road.

The Monega was popular with cattle drovers seeking an alternative to the steep Devil's Elbow that rises between Glen Shee and Braemar, and it also enjoyed royal patronage: in 1861 Queen Victoria crossed on a pony during a stay at Balmoral.

Over time, the Monega fell out of use as the lower-level Tolmounth Road between Clova and Braemar gained favour with drovers and traders. Thereafter, with traffic light, it was used by cattle rustlers and picked up a reputation for smuggling, doubtless witnessing many clandestine movements in its long history.

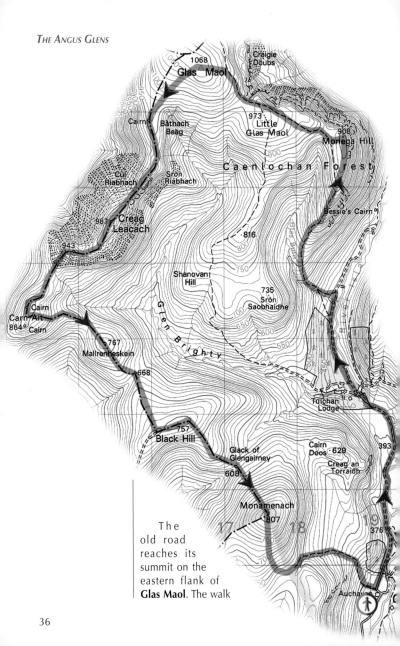

1068
Glas Maol

Craigie
Doubs

Cairn

Bàthach
Beag

973
Little
Glas Maol

908
Monega Hill

Cúl
Riabhach

Sròn
Riabhach

Caenlochan Forest

987
Creag
Leacach

943

Bessie's Cairn

816

750

Shanovant
Hill

735
Sròn
Saobhaidhe

Cairn
Carn Ait
864
Cairn

700

650

600

550

767
Mallrenheskein

Glen Brighty

668

Tulchan
Lodge

757
Black Hill

Glack of
Glengairney

Cairn
Deos

629

Creag an
Torraidh

393

608

17

18

19

Monamenach
807

376

The
old road
reaches its
summit on the
eastern flank of
Glas Maol. The walk

Auchav

branches left and heads west over open hillside to the trig point and stone shelter atop the day's first Munro.

Caenlochan Glen, a remote valley where scarce plants thrive

> The summit of **Glas Maol** affords excellent views north to the Cairngorm mountains. Closer to home, near neighbours Cairn of Claise and Carn an Tuirc – both Munros – lie to the east while the day's next goal, Creag Leacach, awaits to the southwest.

Following the county boundary, marked by an indistinct line of metal fence posts, descend in a southwest direction across open hillside to a prominent cairn at the northern end of a stone wall. This wall, and an accompanying fence, are handy navigational aids as they lead all the way on to the summit of Creag Leacach.

Beyond the narrow entrance, the shelter accommodates two and is a useful refuge from the elements, although not suitable for overnight stays.

Following the wall, the route descends gently to a col where a tiny stone howff (shelter) lurks amid the rocks, to the left of the wall. ▸

From the howff, the route rises over the northern flank of **Creag Leacach**. The ascent is easy at first but soon becomes more arduous, the path weaving a course up through scattered rock and scree to the summit cairn. With slopes falling away steeply on both sides, the summit feels wonderfully exposed.

Continue south and then west along the stony ridge, taking care to avoid rusty fence wire that litters the ground, to reach the southwest top and, from here, set a course for **Carn Ait**, an outlier to the southwest, boasting some impressive cairns.

From Carn Ait descend east on heathery vehicle tracks and then walk southeast over the low mound of **Mallrenheskein** to **Black Hill**, negotiating some deep peat hags in the col between the two. From Black Hill descend to **Glack of Glengairney** and prepare for 200m of fairly remorseless ascent to the summit of **Monamenach**, a Corbett.

Reward for this end of the day effort is a **stunning vista** of the route in its entirety. Glas Maol and Creag Leacach appear very different in character and complexity from this elevated angle but are neighbours nonetheless, while Monega Hill to the east seems a long way off now.

The rocky spine of Creag Leacach cuts across the skyline

A clear path descends the southern flank of Monamenach, joining a good track further down the slope. This descends east to meet the valley track at **Auchavan**.

Monamenach from Creag Leacach

WALK 2
Badandun Hill

Start/Finish	Forestry Commission car park at Freuchies, 2km east of Kirkton of Glenisla on minor road signed for Glenmarkie Lodge (NO 224 608)
Distance	22km (13¾ miles)
Time	6hr
Height gain	708m (2325ft)
Maps	OS 1:50,000 Landranger 43 and 44; OS 1:25,000 Explorer 381 and 388

To truly appreciate the lie of the land in Glen Isla, a hike over Badandun Hill is highly recommended. The summit offers fine vistas across both the fertile lower section of the valley and the wilder upper reaches of the glen, where high peaks cut across the skyline.

Starting from the car park at Freuchies, the route approaches Badandun Hill from the south, crossing green pastures before venturing on to rougher grouse moor. Tracks and paths are generally very good, although accurate navigation is required if visibility is poor on the summit. Underfoot the terrain is good with only occasional boggy patches of ground and some peat hags to negotiate on the summit approach. Dogs should be kept under close control due to the presence of grazing sheep and cattle and ground-nesting birds.

On the north side of the car park, go left and follow a forest road signed for 'Glen Prosen and Glen Clova by Kilbo Path'. The track rises gently through a plantation of pine and larch trees where, during the summer, flowering broom bushes add a generous splash of yellow to the proceedings.

Follow the track for 1km to reach a wooden gate on the left. Go through this and pass through another gate a few metres further on. The route crosses a wooden bridge spanning the outflow of **Loch Shandra** and strikes across the embankment at the southern end of this reservoir. Head for a corrugated iron boathouse at the far end of the

embankment, savouring views north towards Badandun Hill.

Behind the boathouse the embankment path meets a track. Turn right and follow this along the west side of the loch. Approaching the north end of Loch Shandra, where small pockets of woodland hug the shoreline, look out for heron, swans and wildfowl in the reeds.

Leaving the loch behind, the track fords a tiny stream and arrives at a junction with a Cateran Trail marker post. Bear right here, off the marked trail, and follow a grassy track round to a gate. Go though and a rough trail crosses a muddy stream gully before rising over grazing land. ▶

At the top of the field, the track

Badandun Hill mirrored in the calm waters of Loch Shandra

Over to the right are the ruins of Craignity, an abandoned farm, while to the left there is a good view of Mount Blair.

Map continues on page 42

passes through a metal gate and continues across a second field. As it approaches a wall and fence, it swings right and rises to a pair of wooden gates at the top left-hand corner of the field. Go through the right-hand gate and a track leads to a derelict farmhouse and outbuildings at **Craighead**.

Follow the track through the farmyard. At the far end pass through a gate, swing right and climb to a high gate above a wooden shed. Go through the gate and turn right to enter a strip of grassland separating tall Scots pine and larch trees on the left and a younger plantation of spruce to the right.

Head north through this grassy ride and at the end of the trees continue on an obvious track across the broad moorland ridge. The track rises gently before dipping to pass through a gate in a stone wall. Here the real work begins.

Snaking vehicle tracks serving a line of grouse butts offer one alternative, while following a nearby fence provides a more direct route to a prominent cairn at the southern end of the summit ridge. The ascent is initially strenuous but eases as the line of the ridge approaches. To the south views open out over Loch Shandra while to the west Auchintaple Loch can be clearly seen, with Mount Blair behind.

Once on the ridge a pleasant elevated stroll awaits. A narrow path follows the line of an old fence, crossing heather hillside and dipping into the occasional peat bog, where mountain hare and grouse lurk. As the summit nears, the peaty hags become more extensive but the path weaves a reasonably good route through them, rising on to firmer terrain to join a track by a wall. The track leads up to the summit of **Badandun Hill**, marked by a trig point and a small cairn.

Stay on the track as it descends the northeast flank of the hill to the col below Craig Lair then head west, contouring round the slope to join a good track that leads down through the valley, entering woodland above a steading at Fergus.

The track descends to **Fergus** but just before the building is reached, go left and cross a burn by a footbridge just upstream from a ford. Once over, a good track

The track to Badandun Hill offers a well-graded approach

strikes south, leading down Glen Isla to a cottage at **Dail na Sneachd**. Skirting between the bulk of Badandun Hill to the left and the delicate ribbon of the River Isla to the right, the track continues for a further 2.5km, crossing open pasture before meeting the public road by a bridge spanning the River Isla in the hamlet of **Little Forter**.

Walk 300m south along the road and then branch left, crossing a ladder stile to join a track (part of the Cateran Trail). Follow this up to a junction and turn right to reach **Auchintaple Loch**, a hidden gem of calm water with a fine view of Badandun Hill.

The track ends just beyond a sturdy boatshed but a path continues round the water, passing through two gates and crossing an embankment at the southern end of the loch. A little further on, stepping-stones adjacent to a short length of wood-and-wire-mesh fence negotiate the outflow and, on the other side, a narrow line in the heather leads up to a gate and ladder stile, where the route rejoins the Cateran Trail.

Cross the stile and follow the track south to a junction. Go left and the track contours round the hillside, rising to a gate. Just prior to the gate, branch right, following a grassy path down the heathery slope to a gate and stile.

The path continues from here down to the base of the valley where a stream is crossed before the way heads over open moor, leading back to **Loch Shandra** and its boathouse. Retrace steps from here back to **Freuchies**.

Badandun Hill from Auchintaple Loch

WALK 3
Mount Blair

Start/Finish	Lay-by 300m north of Altaltan and 5km north of Kirkton of Glenisla on B951 (NO 182 638)
Distance	6km (3¾ miles)
Time	3hr
Height gain	500m (1640ft)
Maps	OS 1:50,000 Landranger 43; OS 1:25,000 Explorer 387

Mount Blair is one of the best viewpoints in Angus and in good weather an impressively diverse panorama of mountains and hills can be seen from the top.

The most direct route up is via a track rising over the northern slope from the B951 road near Cray. It is, however, a rather uninspiring plod over grassy pasture and heather moor. This route comes in from the east with a more scenic approach but it presents a steep early climb and some sections of path are indistinct, requiring careful navigation over a slope peppered with rocks and crags. The ground is generally firm with only a couple of patches of boggy ground to negotiate. Some uneven terrain is crossed on the descent. Dogs should be kept under close control due to the presence of grazing sheep and ground-nesting birds.

At the northern end of the lay-by, to the left of a pair of metal gates, cross a simple wooden stile and head across flat grass between trees. Ascend the slope of grass and heather beyond and aim for a lone tree on the hillside above. Continue up the slope for 20m from this tree and then bear left on a narrow stony path that rises on to an obvious shoulder.

45

Mount Blair rising above woodland on its northwest flank

Once on the shoulder, bear right and follow an indistinct grassy trail that meets a more obvious path higher up. This rises north between two lone trees, the higher of the pair clinging to a rocky crag. Pass below this tree and carry on along the path, heading north below **Creag na Cuigeil**.

When the path peters out, bear left up the slope to join another narrow trail that leads north to a small rocky outcrop. Curve left here and an equally narrow but more obvious path zigzags up the slope, becoming clearer as height is gained.

The ascent through heather and blaeberry bushes is arduous but height is gained quickly and magnificent views open out, particularly to the northeast over 16th-century Forter Castle and up Glen Isla towards the mountains of Glas Maol and Creag Leacach.

Originally built in 1560, four-storey **Forter Castle** was the fortified home of the Ogilvies, descendants of the ancient Earls of Angus. However, in 1640 the Campbells of Inverewe, on the instructions of the Eighth Earl of Argyll, stormed the building, along with Airlie Castle, another home of the Ogilvie clan. The building soldiered on briefly for a time but it never recovered from the attack and slowly fell into ruin.

Derelict and abandoned, the tower house was bought in 1988 for the princely sum of £15,000. Restored to its former glory and now offering luxury holiday lets, it is a shining example of a ruinous historic structure gaining a new lease of life.

The path weaves up to a small cairn perched on the end of the ridge above Creag na Cuigeil. Walk southwest from here, the trail following a line of fence posts across heathery hillside to dark peat hags that mark the start of the final ascent to the top of **Mount Blair**, a Graham.

A sturdy telecommunications mast dominates the summit. Below this there is a trig point, a large cairn and a neatly constructed **stone shelter-cum-viewpoint indicator**. For many years, a set of metal panels guided the eye in the direction of the 37 Munros visible on a clear day. They include Ben

The view north up Glen Isla from Mount Blair towards Caenlochan Glen and the mountains above

The memorial plaque on the summit

Keep a watchful eye out for rabbit holes that could play havoc with the ankles of unwary walkers.

More and Stob Binnein, over 80km to the west. Unfortunately the panels have since disappeared. One element that has survived is a memorial panel within the shelter carrying small plaques with the names of those for whom this was a particularly treasured spot.

From the summit, pass to the left of the mast and descend south on a path that runs parallel with a wall to reach a fence and stile. Do not cross the stile but turn left, following the fence down over open hillside, Corrie Vanoch up to the left. There is a path of sorts but the terrain underfoot is uneven, so careful placing of the feet is required.

Further down the slope the fence makes a sharp right-hand turn and continues over rough ground to reach more refined pasture. Cross a wooden section of fence, turn left and head down the grassy slope, keeping the fence to the left. There are a couple of boggy streams to negotiate. ◄

In the base of the valley, the fence bears left. Keep to the right of an older fence at this point and follow grassy vehicle tracks as they ford a shallow stream. Stay with the old fence but be prepared to detour right briefly to avoid some marshy ground.

The fence continues to a metal gate. Pass through this and turn right to join a good track that descends west, curving left above a small plantation before turning right for the final short stretch down to meet the B951. Once on the road, turn left and follow it to the lay-by.

WALK 4
Mealna Letter

Start/Finish	Small lay-by on Angus/Perthshire boundary, 1km east of Cray on B951 (NO 153 642)
Distance	12.5km (7¾ miles)
Time	3hr 30min
Height gain	475m (1560ft)
Maps	OS 1:50,000 Landranger 43; OS 1:25,000 Explorer 387

Mealna Letter – also known as Duchray Hill – straddles the border between Angus and the neighbouring county of Perthshire.

Initially riding the boundary line from the base of the valley to the summit, the route then descends the northern slopes of Mealna Letter, a Graham, to Loch Beanie, a pool of upland water lying in hilly folds above Glen Beanie. Dropping into Glen Shee, the walk links up with the Cateran Trail for the return leg. While the higher ground offers solid terrain, some wet and boggy ground must be negotiated, particularly on the initial approach to Mealna Letter and below Loch Beanie. Significant stretches follow narrow or indistinct paths or are pathless. Good navigation skills are therefore a must. Dogs should be kept under close control due to the presence of grazing sheep.

Walk 100m east on the B951 to a metal gate on the left-hand side of the road, adjacent to the eastern edge of a large commercial forestry plantation. Go through the gate and head north over rough pasture, following the edge of the plantation closely. The going is mixed, firm in places and boggy in parts, particularly where large swathes of reeds grow. ▶

A vague path leads to a second metal gate. Beyond this and a patch of spongy moss, the way becomes clearer, ascending on to firmer ground. Although grazed by sheep and deer, wild flowers, purple thistles and pink heather grow well here, adding splashes of colour to the slope during the summer months.

The climb quickly becomes more strenuous, the route rising to meet a fence running parallel with a wall.

Gaiters are recommended after periods of rain when the long grass holds water and can quickly saturate trousers.

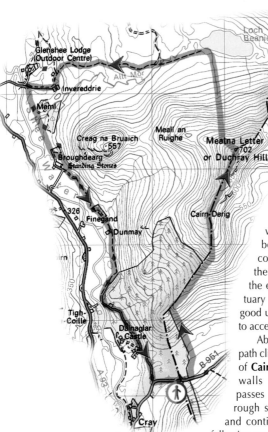

Bear right at this point and follow the fence up the southern ridge of Mealna Letter. While much of the plantation to the left has been felled in recent years, clumps of pine trees remain alongside the wall, which marks the boundary between the county of Perthshire, to the west, and Angus, to the east. These offer sanctuary to red deer that make good use of gaps in the wall to access the open hillside.

Above the plantation, the path climbs steadily to the top of **Cairn Derig**, where three walls meet and the fence passes through a gap in the rough stonework. Bear right and continue along the ridge, following a wall on the left that runs parallel with the path. Enjoying a more relaxed gradient profile, the trail roams along a grassy crest peppered with rock. At its highest point, the wall swings right. To the west sits **Mealna Letter**'s summit cairn, a gap in the dyke enabling easy access.

From the top, there is a **superb view** northwest up Glen Shee towards the clustered Munros of Glas Tulaichean, Carn an Righ and Beinn Iutharn Mhor. To the south the most prominent natural landmark is Mount Blair. Closer to hand, in the valley below,

is Loch Beanie and, across the water, Craigenloch Hill and, behind it, Monamenach.

The tranquil waters of Loch Beanie nestle below Craigenloch Hill

The descent to **Loch Beanie** is across open hillside, grassy in the main but with a few small easy-to-avoid patches of scattered rock. Head north and aim for a small hut close to the western end of the loch. A narrow path can be found as the loch is neared and this leads directly to the wooden hut – a locked boathouse sitting on the edge of the water.

A grassy track, frequently boggy, heads west from the hut. It leads down to a wooden gate and, below this, a wooden bridge spanning the **Allt Mor**. Cross the bridge and bear left, an obvious path rising on to a grassy embankment. Continue on this path, which is very indistinct in parts, heading over open higher ground and away from the Allt Mor. ▶

Careful navigation is required on this next stretch.

When a strung-out line of Scots pine trees running alongside a rundown wall comes into view, aim for a lone tree at the southern end of the line. The route passes through a gate in a high fence and, beyond this (and with the lone tree still offering guidance), crosses through a gap in the wall. A faint track descends from here, passing through a gate to meet a better track close to farm

On the Cateran Trail

buildings. Follow this south towards **Invereddrie** where the track swings west to meet the Cateran Trail, which bisects it.

Turn left and follow the waymarked path south through Glen Shee, crossing a mix of rough pasture and arable land. The trail passes below a prominent Celtic cross, located atop a mound to the left, before crossing the Allt Mor once again at a bridge.

The trail rises over an embankment and continues to a junction by a gate just north of **Broughdearg Farm**. Bear left and the track loops up to a wooden ladder stile spanning a wall below a short telecommunications mast. Cross over and, on the other side, turn right, following a very rough path that runs parallel with the wall to another ladder stile. Climb over the stile and descend to meet a good track. Turn left and walk south.

Behind the farm steading at **Dunmay**, the next building encountered, bear left and, at a pond beyond, turn left to go through a high wooden gate. The trail strikes across bracken-covered hillside to another gate after which the path skirts below coniferous woodland to meet

Dalnaglar Castle was built in the 19th century on the site of an earlier stronghold

a track by a high wall. Turn left to enter the grounds of **Dalnaglar Castle**.

Rising past a cottage on the left, the track swings right at the next junction and, a little further on, passes the whitewashed castle. ▶

Beyond the castle, the track emerges on to a surfaced road serving both the castle and estate cottages. Go left and follow the road for 500m to meet the B951. Following a Cateran Trail sign for Glen Isla, turn left and walk east on the B951 to return to the start point.

Although not open to the public, it is a venue for weddings and outdoor pursuits such as stalking and fishing.

WALK 5
Craigie Thieves

Start/Finish	Car park at Backwater Reservoir dam, 1.5km north of junction of B951 and B954, Glen Isla (NO 251 590)
Distance	25km (15½ miles)
Time	6hr 30min
Height gain	786m (2580ft)
Maps	OS 1:50,000 Landranger 44 and 53; OS 1:25,000 Explorer 381 and 388

Backwater Reservoir is a popular escape for walkers seeking a few pleasant hours in the countryside. Lying just off the main road through Glen Isla, an undemanding circuit loops its shoreline, offering a taste of the solitude that lies beyond. Few venture far from the water, leaving the upper reaches of Glen Damff largely undisturbed. There are no high peaks here, just wild lands and an airy sense of freedom.

From the northern end of the reservoir, the route follows estate tracks and paths over heather moor on the western side of the glen to the summit of Craigie Thieves. Returning over the top of a ridge on the eastern side of the valley, trails hewn from the heather to access lines of grouse butts ensure effortless navigation. The terrain is generally firm. Dogs should be kept under close control due to the presence of grazing sheep and ground-nesting birds. The route crosses a working grouse moor.

Leave the car park, cross the road, pass between stone gateposts and head north on a surfaced track that runs along the west side of the reservoir. It passes below a house and leads briefly through woodland before running above open ground offering good views across the water and north up Glen Damff.

Although the project to build **Backwater Reservoir** was initiated by Dundee Corporation in 1964, it was completed by the newly created East of Scotland Water Board and is now operated by Scottish Water. Opened by Queen Elizabeth II in 1969, the reservoir

The view north over Backwater Reservoir

supplies water to 300,000 people. The dam was the first in Britain to use chemical grouting to create a waterproof barrier below the embankment.

With a solid track underfoot, the walking is easy. The next significant landmark, on the right, is a waterside chalet used by anglers. Beyond this the track is engulfed by woodland once again.

The trees are but a brief interlude, and beyond a gate the track leads across a field. At the far end it curves right and then left, rising towards forestry. Continue until you reach a junction; branch right on a path signed for Glen Damff. The path enters a plantation of pine and larch and leads to a gate on the northern edge of the woodland.

Go through and a rutted track running alongside an old wall descends across grazing land. There are a couple of gates to negotiate on the way down before a wooden bridge spanning the Glendamff Burn is reached at the bottom of the slope. ▶

The ground immediately before the bridge is marshy.

Cross the bridge and head up to a gate in a wall to join a track. Turn left and walk north, following the **Glendamff Burn** upstream. (For a shorter day out, turn right at this point and return to the Backwater dam via Glenhead Farm.) Track and stream converge on three

55

separate occasions in quick succession. A sturdy wooden footbridge provides the first crossing while a pair of metal girders slung over the water a few metres below a ford offers safe passage at the second crossing. At the third crossing point, there is a flat wooden bridge.

Map continues on page 57

The way negotiates scattered agricultural fencing to reach a metal gate. Beyond this, grassy tracks fork. Take the route on the left and, flanked by dense woodland to the left, begin a long but sedate ascent to the top of **Cairn Daunie**.

The track peters out on the summit and the walk continues over open hillside, following a high deer fence all the way to the top of **Craigie Thieves**.

At 689m high – and the most northerly point of the route – this hill may not be big but it does offer a **grandstand view** across Glen Prosen to the Munros of Driesh and Mayar.

Swapping the east side of Glen Damff for the west, descend southeast from the summit, following a fence down to a cairn and continue on the same course to the top of **The High Tree**, an elevated spot with a vista over Glen Prosen.

Walk south from here, a clear route descending over the crest of a well-defined ridge to **Bad Buidhe**, where a prominent cairn stands by the track, overlooking the valley below. Across the valley, to the south, Hare Cairn dominates the view.

The descent into the base of the glen follows tracks cut through the heather to access the grouse moors. A reasonably direct route can be found, leading down to a point where a more obvious track fords the **Glendamff Burn**.

There are two water crossings to be made – the first entails a short jump from the bank to a large stone located a couple of metres upstream from the ford while the second is equally straightforward, a scattering of stones affording a dry crossing. The track pulls away from the stream, striking a straight line over grassland where sheep usually graze. It passes a small fenced enclosure before continuing to meet the track that was followed on to Cairn Daunie at the fork above the metal gate.

Head back down the glen, making the trio of stream crossings once again, to return to the gate in the stone wall encountered on the outward route. Continue straight ahead at this point, following the track past a wooden shed lying within a walled enclosure and, beyond a gate, a derelict cottage at **Barny**. ▶

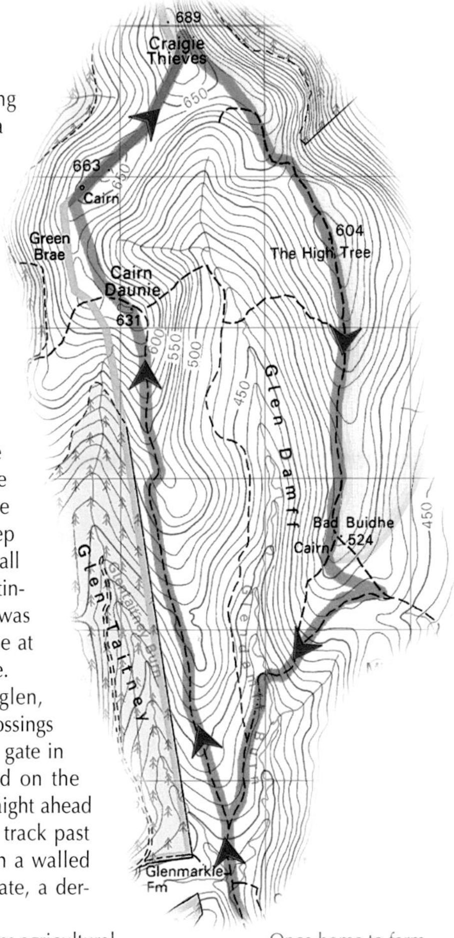

The track continues across agricultural land, a mix of pasture and crops. It passes farm sheds before curving east around the wooded southern slopes of Cuilt Hill to reach **Glenhead Farm**.

At the next junction, beyond a cottage, turn right to join the public road. This descends to cross the Hole Burn before striking a course along the eastern side of **Backwater Reservoir**. Cross the dam at the southern end of the water to return to the car park.

Once home to farm workers this has now been reduced to a store for hay and animal feeds.

The following labels appear on the map:

. 689
Craigie Thieves
663 . Cairn
Green Brae
604 The High Tree
Cairn Daunie 631
Glen Damff
Glen Tairney
Bad Buidhe Cairn 524
Glenmarkie Fm

WALK 6
Corwharn and Milldewan Hill

Start/Finish	Car park on eastern side of Backwater Reservoir, 5.5km north of junction of B591 and B954 in Glen Isla, below Little Ley (NO 256 614)
Distance	15km (9¼ miles)
Time	4hr 15min
Height gain	515m (1690ft)
Maps	OS 1:50,000 Landranger 44; OS 1:25,000 Explorer 381 and 388

Lying between Glen Isla and Glen Prosen, Corwharn and Milldewan Hill combine to offer a fine upland circuit from the Backwater Reservoir, with excellent views over both valleys.

The route begins at a public car park close to the northern end of the reservoir and approaches via a track linking Isla and Prosen. It rises through pleasant swathes of woodland before open hillside beckons. Navigation is straightforward. On high ground, there are paths and stalkers' tracks while fence lines offer a useful additional aid in poor visibility. The terrain is generally very good although peaty ground with some easily avoided boggy ground must be negotiated on the open hillside. Dogs should be kept under close control due to the presence of grazing sheep and ground-nesting birds. The route crosses a working grouse moor.

Set off from the car park, which has a pleasant picnic area overlooking Backwater Reservoir, and walk north along the minor road for 1.5km to **Glenhead Farm**. The road curves down to cross Hole Burn by a bridge sitting amid a cluster of stone and maroon-coloured corrugated iron agricultural sheds – one of which has a white bird painted on its roof – before climbing to a junction adjacent to a cottage lying to the east of the farm.

Turn right and, following a sign for 'Glen Prosen', walk along a good track that passes below a second cottage and by a wooden shed before leading on through a metal gate where a prominent notice asks dog owners to keep their pets on a lead. The way rises gently round the lower slopes of **Cuilt Hill**, curving north to follow Hole Burn upstream. ▶

The track leads north over pasture and below a plantation on the left to a derelict stone barn at **Hole**. A little way beyond this, it crosses a stream by a concrete bridge and passes through a metal gate to reach a junction. Turn right here, climb through a second metal gate, and the track heads up over open ground, skirting the fringes of woodland. The route here is rutted and can be boggy in wet weather.

Beyond another gate, the track strikes out over hillside, rising to a wooden gate on the western perimeter of **Drumshade Plantation**.

Despite its commercial roots, Drumshade is a pleasure to walk through, an airy mix of Scots pine, larch and spruce where, for those who go quietly, it is not uncommon to spot both **red and roe deer** lurking amongst the trees.

The track climbs steadily to cross a small stream. On the other side, bear right and cross a grassy track running

Ahead the rounded summit of Corwharn can be seen poking its head up above a blanket of forestry.

A sheltered track carpeted with pine needles rises through Drumshade Plantation

Expect to negotiate some fallen timber, particularly after windy weather, although this is regularly cleared.

at right angles across the route. Beyond this junction, the track curves to the left and rises more steeply. ◀

The track emerges on to open moor at a wooden gate at the top of the plantation. Continue on the track for another 500m, following it as it dips to cross a stream gully. At the next bend, branch right over heathery hillside, heading for a wooden gate at a junction of fences.

Clamber over the gate and follow a narrow trail up over open hillside. The route runs parallel with a fence and, as higher ground is reached, the path offers a good line through a series of peat hags and around marshy patches of ground.

On a clear day, there are **excellent views** north over Glen Prosen towards the hills above Glen Clova and Glen Doll. Particularly prominent are the deep corries occupied by Loch Brandy and Loch Wharrel.

A pillar cairn on Corwharn surveys the surrounding landscape

Approaching the top of **Corwharn**, the route reaches a pair of wooden gates at a meeting point of fences. Turn right and follow the fence running southwest on to the summit of the hill.

While there is no cairn on the top, several metres to the east there stands a prominent column of stone. Beautifully pieced together and around two metres in height, it enjoys a commanding view over the valley below.

Known as a **'stone man'**, cairns of this type are common in these parts. The hills around nearby Glen Damff are peppered with them while Hill of Strone, to the north of Corwharn, has

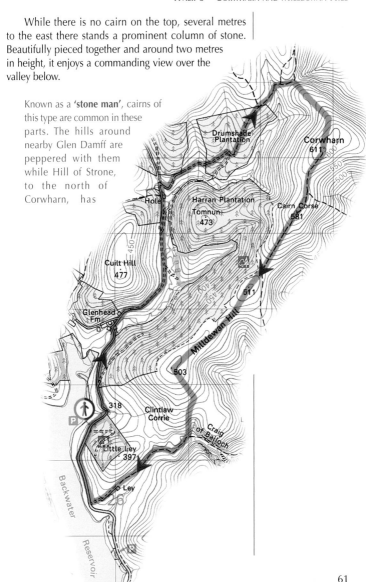

stone men occupying its eastern flank. Why they were constructed is not exactly known. They may just be the work of stonemasons intent on showing off their skills.

Leave the summit and descend southwest on to the unmarked summit of **Cairn Corse**. The fence remains as a helpful navigational aid. Continue on the same line and the route descends into a shallow dip before rising effortlessly on to the summit of **Milldewan Hill**.

A pleasant upland tramp leads from here over the long spine of the hill, a track cut through the heather swinging left at the end of the ridge, descending alongside a fence. At the base of the initial slope, where the gradient eases noticeably, cross the fence to the right and pick up a path leading in the direction of Craig of Balloch. Where it swings right, branch left, aiming for a narrow stream gully that cuts through the slope, heading down past a lone tree and into a ravine.

The narrow gorge of **Craig of Balloch**, flanked on either side by crags and steep banks of rock and scree is a hidden gem, its rough, unrefined edges a striking contrast to the rounded hills above.

The base of the glen is marshy but a grassy track offers a dry course west, leading from Craig of Balloch towards Backwater Reservoir. The way crosses open hillside then two fields of pasture, passing a ruined barn and enclosures at **Ley**, before descending to a gate, beyond which the route rejoins the road running along the eastern side of the reservoir.

Turn right and walk north along the road for the final 1km.

WALK 7
Craigie Law and Crock

Start/Finish	Forestry Commission car park at Freuchies, 2km east of Kirkton of Glenisla on minor road signed for Glenmarkie Lodge (NO 224 608)
Distance	15km (9¼ miles)
Time	4hr
Height gain	440m (1445ft)
Maps	OS 1:50,000 Landranger 44; OS 1:25,000 Explorer 381 and 388

This is a sheltered forest walk ideal for days when the weather is not so good and some natural protection from the elements is in order.

Starting from the car park at Freuchies the route ascends the neighbouring hills of Craigie Law and Crock. Both are heavily wooded but with clear, well-graded tracks and paths throughout, navigation is simple. The underfoot conditions are generally very good, although some of the higher sections of path within the forest can be boggy. After stormy conditions, expect to encounter fallen trees. There are excellent panoramas when the route emerges on to the domed summit of Crock.

Leave the car park by its main entrance, turn left and head north on a surfaced minor road, following signs for Glenmarkie Lodge. The road climbs steeply at first but the gradient soon eases and it rises more gently round the eastern flank of **Cairn Hill**, curving left to head north, bounded on either side by trees.

The single-track road continues to a junction 2.5km from the start. Branch left at this point and follow a good forest track up through the plantation. The way rises above **Glenmarkie Lodge**, a guesthouse with a horse riding centre and spa.

Managed by Forestry Commission Scotland, **Glen Isla Forest** is a commercial plantation with a network of tracks and paths that have long been enjoyed by walkers, cyclists and, in the winter months, cross-country skiers. The longest of the tracks, which extends north through Glen Finlet, provides a useful link between Glen Isla and Glen Prosen for those on foot or two wheels.

The track pulls up through the trees, rising over the eastern slopes of both Crock and Craigie Law. Due to the blanket of forestry, however, there is little to see of either summit from this angle.

The route crosses two areas where the older trees have been felled, offering a pleasant open outlook over the valley below, before curving left around the northern shoulder of **Craigie Law**. At the next corner, where the track makes a sharp right-hand turn and descends north, go left to join a path leading into the trees.

Running alongside a stubby moss and lichen-encrusted wall, the way rises north through a shady woodland corridor. Underfoot, it can be muddy and there is plenty of evidence to indicate the route is well used by pony trekkers from Glenmarkie Lodge – droppings and hoof prints pepper the ground. Step carefully! The woodland on either side is dense and the canopy above thick but chinks of light somehow manage to filter through. ◄

The summit of **Craigie Law** is not marked in any obvious way and is so indiscernible that the best indication it

The path is at its most striking when there is warm sunshine after rain, the rising vapours creating a fairytale fog.

has been reached is when the path begins to descend. It drops gently, remaining confined within the conifers as it continues its course south. Thanks to some felling in recent years it emerges briefly from the trees to cross the shallow col between Craigie Law and Crock.

There is, however, no escaping the forest and on the far side of the clearing, the path re-enters the plantation and, carpeted in pine needles, embarks upon a fairly stiff pull up. At the top of this second leafy tunnel, daylight signals the arrival of open hillside: a great pear-shaped tract of heather moor, encircled by the forest. Despite the best efforts of some stray saplings to secure a foothold, it remains an oasis of open space.

Vague trails penetrate the heather and navigation to the top of **Crock** is easy – just walk uphill until the small summit cairn is reached.

Sitting high above the tallest of the trees, **uninterrupted views** open out in all direction. To the north, the peaks rising from Glen Isla and Glen Clova are visible on a clear day while to the west Mount Blair is an easily distinguished landmark. To the south, vistas extend over Glen Isla and the fertile Vale of Strathmore towards the North Sea.

Craigie Law and Crock, hills clad in commercial forestry

65

The moorland summit of Crock offers a welcome escape from the surrounding forestry

An obvious path drops south from the top, heading towards an opening in the trees at the bottom of the clearing. The route descends from here with vigour, loosing height swiftly as it canters down the southern shoulder of Crock.

Lower down, a junction is reached. Turn right at this point and follow a clear path that curves right and heads north, contouring along the western slope of Crock to meet a forest road, 2.5km further on, at the end of a patch of felled ground.

Turn left and follow the track south. Passing above another felled area, it pops in and out of the trees before swinging round the slope to **Tulloch**, a remote cottage perched high on the hillside and boasting a wonderful view over Loch Shandra in the base of the valley.

Beyond Tulloch, the track descends towards the southern end of the loch. The reservoir lies just off route but a short detour can be made by passing through a wooden gate on the right at the bottom of the slope. Beyond a second gate, a bridge spans the outflow, leading on to the embankment dam.

From **Loch Shandra**, the track continues south. Buffeted by broom bushes it cuts a straight course through the lower, less intense fringes of the plantation, running parallel with a gurgling little stream to **Freuchies**.

GLEN PROSEN

Glentarie Cottage, Glen Tarie (Walk 10)

WALK 8

*Tulloch Hill, The Goal
and Hill of Couternach*

Start/Finish	Tulloch Hill car park, 2km west of Dykehead on Glen Prosen road (NO 371 606)
Distance	14km (8¾ miles)
Time	4hr
Height gain	500m (1640ft)
Maps	OS 1:50,000 Landranger 44; OS 1:25,000 Explorer 381 and 388

This exhilarating ridge walk over a series of low hills crosses the high ground between the glens of Clova and Prosen and boasts some spectacular views of both. There are good tracks and paths for the majority of the route and a section of road walking at the end. Navigation is straightforward. With little in the way of natural shelter beyond the woodlands on Tulloch Hill, the high ground is exposed to the elements. The terrain is very good with only a few boggy spots. Dogs should be kept under close control due to the presence of grazing sheep and ground-nesting birds.

Adjacent to an information board in the car park, a track – signed as the footpath to Airlie Monument – sets off, rising through tall pine trees. Accompanied by occasional waymarker posts with yellow arrows, the route curves left and then right, crossing grassy ground dotted with purple foxgloves.

The ascent is quite strenuous but further up the slope the gradient eases as the way contours round the hillside to reach a junction. ◄ Turn left here and the track rises gently, curving right as it climbs to the top of the woodland. The way emerges from the trees below Airlie Monument (also known as the Airlie Memorial Tower).

There are some muddy patches to contend with on this section.

AIRLIE MEMORIAL TOWER

One of the most prominent landmarks in Angus, this red sandstone tower stands 30m high and cost £1300 to build. A category B listed building, it is visible from many miles around, and were it possible to enter the tower and climb to the top it would doubtless afford stunning vistas. It was erected in 1901 to commemorate the life of David William Stanley Ogilvy, the Ninth Earl of Airlie, who died in battle on 11 June 1900 while leading his regiment, the 12th Lancers, at Diamond Hill, near Pretoria, during the Boer War. He was 44.

The Earl was a distinguished soldier who fought in the Afghan War (1878–79), in Suakim (1884), in Sudan (1884–85) and in the Boer War (1899–1900). He was wounded three times during his military career and was mentioned in dispatches on numerous occasions.

Sturdy metal doors prevent entry to the tower, although visitors are welcome during the annual Doors Open Day event, held in the autumn. Even when viewed from below it is, however, an impressive structure, with some ornate carved panels set into the stonework.

From the tower, a grassy track strikes north over **Tulloch Hill**. It runs level across a broad ridge of heather, grass and blaeberry bushes to a wooden gate and ladder stile. Go through the gate – the stile is rickety – and

Tulloch Hill and the landmark Airlie Memorial Tower seen from The Goal

continue north, enjoying views across Glen Clova to Glen Moy, to the right, and Glen Prosen, to the left. The track descends gently into a dip. The upper fringes of pine forest to the left are a good place to spot roe deer that have emerged from the trees to graze the open hillside.

From the dip, the track rises to a wooden gate at the edge of woodland. Go through this, pass through a gap in a wall beyond and follow a grassy corridor through the trees to another gate and ladder stile. ◄ Cross the stile and descend into a broad clearing, enjoying a brief view over Glen Clova to the summits of Finbracks and Manywee.

Beyond the trees, a rough and ready path rises through a wide corridor of heather moor that cuts between plantations on the

The track here is frequently muddy underfoot.

Glen Clova from Hill of Couternach

left and right. Following a line of wooden fence posts and passing occasional lone pine trees, the path is initially soft and squelching underfoot with easily avoidable boggy spots, but as height is gained it improves markedly. Pause occasionally for views south to Airlie Monument.

At the top of a strenuous incline, the gradient eases and the path strikes a level course, swinging left to reach a stand of weather-beaten pine trees. Pass through a gap in a fence running at right angles to the route where once there was a gate. The main track curves left at this point. Walk straight ahead, following a rougher track over heather moor. The way runs parallel with an old fence line, on the left.

The path – increasingly distinct – passes over the unmarked top of **The Goal**. Beyond the summit, it curves right and descends to the base of the col below, at **Sneck of Corinch**. During the descent, cross the fence – there are gaps where the rusty wires have perished – to pick up a better parallel track.

From the col, a well-graded ascent on a firm track of peat and stone rises on to **Craigs of Lethnot**, the fence on the right remaining by its side. On the broad summit, two small cairns lie to the east of the track. The first marks the summit while the second, supporting a metal cross, is worth seeking out for bird's-eye views of Glen Clova below.

The track dips into another col with occasional easily avoided boggy patches before climbing to the final summit of the route, **Hill of Couternach**. Approaching the top, the route reaches a junction, where the accompanying fence turns right. Go left at this point and the route curves left. The heathery unmarked summit of the hill lies just off the track, from where there are views across Glen Clova to Ben Tirran and the rocky corries of Loch Brandy and Loch Wharral.

Stay on the track as it descends the southwest shoulder of Hill of Couternach. Running parallel with a line of wooden fence posts, the grassy track ends partway down the slope. Continue straight ahead, following the fence line. ◀

Careful footing is required to avoid the often-concealed foundation stones of a former wall and stray lengths of rusty fence wire.

Descend to meet a fence running at right angles in the base of Glen Cally, beyond which there is a stream. Cross the fence and, picking up a narrow trail through grass and reeds, stay to the right of the stream to reach a narrow point a few metres on where the water is crossed in a single stride.

Once over, the narrow path rises through heather to a grassy track. Turn left and follow the track south through Glen Cally. Although not well walked, the route is distinct enough. The track passes a mound of stones on the left and climbs – gently at first and then more stiffly – on to the shoulder below **Cairn Leith**.

Running along above birch woods to the right, the route descends south, following another fence line. Cross this to join a better parallel track and in due course the route curves right and drops more steeply to meet the main road through Glen Prosen, opposite pine woodland.

Turn left and follow the road, normally very quiet, which descends past a whitewashed cottage at **Buckhood** to cross the stream running through Glen Cally by a stone bridge. Flanked by mixed woodland and commercial forestry plantations on the left, it climbs steadily back to the car park, passing above rough pasture grazed by sheep, cattle and rabbits on the right.

WALK 9

Cat Law and Long Goat

Start/Finish	Track end below Turf Hill, 2km southeast of Easter Lednathie on minor road linking Kirriemuir to Glenprosen Village (NO 354 618)
Distance	11km (6¾ miles)
Time	3hr 30min
Height gain	550m (1805ft)
Maps	OS 1:50,000 Landranger 44; OS 1:25,000 Explorer 381 and 388

Lying to the south of Glen Prosen, Cat Law sits on the periphery of the Angus hills, a last bastion of high ground overlooking Vale of Strathmore.

The route begins with a stiff ascent of neighbouring Long Goat – 100m lower – before progressing to the summit, an excellent viewpoint. Hill paths and tracks – rough in places but distinct enough – ensure navigation in all but the worst weather is painless. Estate tracks laid to access grouse moors offer an easy descent. The return leg of the route is along a surfaced farm track and minor road where traffic is generally light. There is some marshy ground to negotiate. Dogs should be kept under close control due to the presence of grazing sheep and ground-nesting birds. The route skirts the fringes of a working grouse moor.

There is no car park at the start of the walk, but there is a generous amount of wide and flat grassy verge on which to leave vehicles. On the south side of the road, pass through a metal gate and a good track rises gently over heather hillside. The route here, while distinct and easy to walk, is not well used and during the summer months particularly the centre line is beset with grass and reeds. ▸

Gaiters are recommended, particularly during spells of wet weather.

The way passes under a line of overhead cables and continues to climb at a relatively effortless gradient to a second metal gate. Pass through this and bear right, following the track through a dip where conditions underfoot can be marshy. Once over, the route rises up the eastern

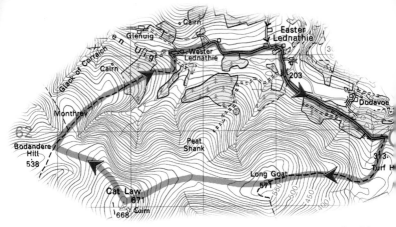

shoulder
of Long Goat and, beyond a swathe of bracken and foxgloves, the ground becomes much firmer.

The route meets a fence coming in from the right and runs parallel with the posts and wire all the way to the top. The ascent is initially steep and strenuous but the gradient eases somewhat as height is gained. The track narrows into a fairly distinct path that leads on to the summit.

> There is no cairn on the top of **Long Goat**. However, adjacent to a wooden gate, there is a small square stone set into the ground. It is an estate boundary marker and one of a number on the route. On a clear day the next peak on the itinerary, Cat Law, is visible to the west.

Remaining on the left side of the fence, descend southwest. A short walk from the summit, at another boundary stone, fence and track curve right, running down the western shoulder of Long Goat.

After a long, gradual descent, the track rises past a wooden gate on the right. It curves left and, with fence still in tow, begins the ascent of Cat Law. On the lower portion of the slope, the route crosses patches of marshy hillside, moist carpets of sphagnum moss indicating soft ground. It is worth veering to the left a little to find

Long Goat and Cat Law from Tulloch Hill (Walk 8)

firmer terrain on heather-clad hillside. Higher up, above a swathe of black peat, the route passes a roofless stone shelter on the right, constructed on a scarping of rock. ▶

Continue up the slope, passing a cairn of white stones above the shelter, and the summit of **Cat Law** is close at hand. The high point lies at a junction of fences where there is a wooden gate and boundary stone.

Follow the fence south to a trio of rundown cairns, one of which offers reasonable shelter from the elements, while Cat Law's trig point is a short hop to the west.

The shelter affords excellent protection from the wind: a good place to pause for a breather or a brew.

There are **panoramic views** from the top. Prominent landmarks include the Airlie Monument to the east, Loch of Lintrathen to the southwest and the town of Kirriemuir to the southeast.

From the junction of fences on the summit, descend over the northwestern shoulder of Cat Law, following a fence and vehicle tracks through the grass, heather and moss. The tracks come and go but the fence remains constant, leading down to meet another fence running at right angles. Cross this to join a solid track on the other side of the wire, in the col between Cat Law and **Bodandere Hill**.

Turn right and walk 200m along the track to a junction. Go right here and follow the track through a wooden gate. Beyond the gate, the track descends rapidly to a metal gate at the top of a woodland of pine and larch. Pass through the gate and stay with the track as it runs down through a corridor separating densely packed stands of commercial spruce.

The track emerges from the trees at a metal gate. Pass through this and continue the descent over pasture, following a wall on the left. Ignore a gap in the wall partway down the slope, where sheep share the grassy pickings with an army of rabbits, and continue down to the bottom of the field. Bear left, passing through a gateway in the wall and vehicle tracks in the grass lead to a metal gate at the end of a row of mature trees.

Enter the farmyard of **Wester Lednathie** at the gate, follow the track over a concrete bridge spanning a stream and turn right. The track leads up past farm sheds to a junction where there are signs for Cat Law and Glen Uig. Ignoring the track for Glen Uig on the left, continue straight ahead, passing kennels and the farmhouse, and cross a cattle grid. The track, sheltered by a line of trees, climbs briefly before flattening off. Cast eyes over the valley for a fine view of Cat Law and then continue along the metalled track to a bench, an equally good spot from which to admire the hill.

The track runs east to a cottage where it swings right, descending towards woodland. Curving left as the trees are approached, it thereafter adopts a straight and level line for the final run to **Easter Lednathie Farm**, where it meets the public road.

Continue straight ahead at the junction and follow the road as it skirts the perimeter of the farm before descending to cross a stone bridge over a stream. The initially easy incline beyond becomes progressively steeper towards the end of the walk.

WALK 10

Knachly and Hill of Spott

Start/Finish	Public car park in Glenprosen Village (NO 328 657)
Distance	10km (6¼ miles)
Time	2hr 45min
Height gain	340m (1115ft)
Maps	OS 1:50,000 Landranger 44; OS 1:25,000 Explorer 388

Accessed from Glenprosen Village, Knachly and Hill of Spott are two low summits easily combined. While a direct ascent of either is possible, this route sets out along the Minister's Road, a long-established right of way crossing the hills between Glen Prosen and Glen Clova. It offers a well-graded ascent on to Balnaboth Moor ahead of an easy climb to the top of Knachly. From there the walk continues on to Hill of Spott before descending back into Glen Prosen where 1.5km of road walking concludes the outing. Navigation is straightforward and there are good tracks and paths for the majority of the way. Dogs should be kept under close control due to the presence of grazing sheep and ground-nesting birds. The route crosses working grouse moor.

The walk starts in a small car park located behind Prosen Church, a pretty little country kirk. Following a sign reading 'Public footpath by the Minister's Road to Glen Clova', take a track striking north from the car park, passing a board with historical information about Balnaboth Moor. ▶ Within a few metres, the route splits three ways. Select the middle track, which curves right and climbs past Pitcarity Cottage to a metal gate.

Beyond the gate, the track crosses rough pasture, passing under a line of overhead cables. Curving left, it rises through a wide bend. Ignore a grassy track coming in from the right and continue up, passing under the overhead cables for a second time.

The route runs along the top of a fenced plantation of pine trees with a fringe of silver birch. It runs parallel with the overhead cables before passing under the wires for

Details of any grouse shooting in the area are posted here during the season.

a third and final time, beyond which there is a wooden gate and adjacent kissing gate. Go through and, ahead, the line of the Minister's Road can be seen crossing the lower slopes of Knachly as it strikes north up Glen Tairie. The track is well defined and the walking easy, evidence that the old road was well constructed.

THE MINISTER'S ROAD

While it is difficult to pin an exact date on when the route was built, it is so named because in the 19th century it was used by ministers appointed to preach at both Prosen Church and Clova Kirk. Based in a manse in Glenprosen Village, the Church of Scotland minister would conduct his first Sunday service at Prosen before heading 6km over the hills to Clova on a pony for his second sermon of the day. The journey was made throughout the year, whatever the weather. Ordnance Survey mapping from the 19th century shows 14 posts along the way, most likely navigational aids.

While there has been a place of worship on the site of Clova Kirk since AD1010, the present church in Glenprosen Village dates from 1802 and replaces an earlier chapel. Both now come under the charge of The Glens and Kirriemuir Old Parish Church in Kirriemuir.

The heritage of the old road is, however, kept alive. Parishioners hold an annual Minister's Walk, beginning with an early afternoon service at Prosen Church and concluding with a service at Clova Kirk.

The Minister's Road rising on to Balnaboth Moor above Glen Prosen

Follow the Minister's Road from the gate up on to Balnaboth Moor. The route rises gently, passing above **Glentairie Cottage**, a former sheep farm and now a holiday let, on the other side of the valley. Underfoot, the track is good with only the occasional easy to avoid muddy spot.

Curving slowly right, the track passes the base of a line of grouse butts before continuing up to a wooden gate at the highest point on the road. To the north, the dramatic corries above Clova are clearly visible.

Do not go through the gate. Instead, turn right and, following a fence, ascend the northern shoulder of Knachly, the summit in view ahead. A track cut through the heather runs parallel with the fence. While the gradient is initially far from strenuous, higher up the slope does becomes steeper. The fence continues to the top of the line of grouse butts encountered earlier. Here it curves left, leading to the top of **Knachly**, marked by a small cairn. The track veers right before the summit is reached.

Descend south over heather hillside, following the fence initially and taking care to avoid a very small rocky outcrop just below the summit. Lower down, it is worth veering right to join an obvious track that leads down into the col between Knachly and Hill of Spott.

Maintain a southern line, passing a wooden gate on the left and a path branching right. The latter offers a useful escape route. It descends to the bottom of a strung-out line of larch trees and continues down to the wooden gate and kissing gate in Glen Tairie.

The patchwork slopes of Hill of Spott from Knachly

From the col, continue straight ahead on the track. It rises over the north flank of **Hill of Spott**, passing through a gate just below the summit, the lower of the route's two high points. A long pleasant elevated hike along the southern ridge of the hill is followed by a steeper descent to **Cairn Leith** where there is an impressive little set of crags and boulders.

Below Cairn Leith, look out for a track running at right angles across the hillside. Once on this, turn right and follow it down into leafy birch woodland where roe deer are often to be found grazing. Grassy underfoot, the track drops gently to meet the Glen Prosen road.

Bear right and follow the road northwest. Traffic is generally very light. Running parallel with Prosen Water, the road leads to a junction by the large house at **Spott**. Continue straight ahead here, the road running between the river, on the left, and fenced arable land, on the right, to reach Prosen Church.

WALK 11

Hill of Strone and Driesh

Start/Finish	Small parking area by bridge over Prosen Water at Glenprosen Lodge 4.5km northwest of Glenprosen Village (NO 294 678)
Distance	20km (12½ miles)
Time	5hr 30min
Height gain	930m (3050ft)
Maps	OS 1:50,000 Landranger 44; OS 1:25,000 Explorer 388

The Munro of Driesh is most frequently climbed from Glen Doll, via the Kilbo Path. This route approaches from Glen Prosen in the south and incorporates neighbouring Hill of Strone, a lower peak.

Ascending via good forest tracks and clear hill paths, careful navigation is required over the summits if visibility is poor. The route returns to Glen Prosen via the Kilbo Path, a long-established and easily followed right of way. The walk concludes with a valley hike along a low-level estate track. The going underfoot is generally very good throughout, although some soft terrain may be encountered on the wooded section of the Kilbo Path. Dogs should be kept under close control due to the presence of grazing sheep and ground-nesting birds.

Cross the road bridge over Prosen Water adjacent to the parking area and follow the road northwest. It climbs past **Glenprosen Lodge**, flattening out to reach a junction. Here the road curves left, descending towards cottages and estate buildings. Leave it at this juncture and continue straight ahead on a track that enters **Glenclova Forest** at a metal gate a few metres further on.

The wide forest track climbs steadily, curving north along the edge of the plantation. Open ground to the left, with views over the remoter upper reaches of Glen Prosen, alleviates the claustrophobia many forest routes impose upon the walker.

As the track progresses, it slowly curves left before swinging round to cross **Dead Water**, an unexpectedly

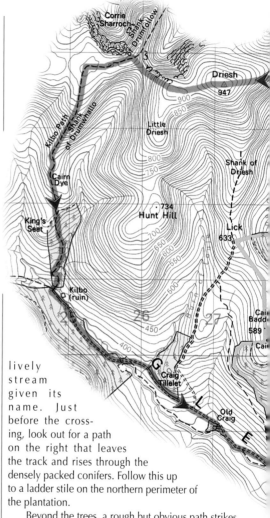

lively
stream
given its
name. Just
before the cross-
ing, look out for a path
on the right that leaves
the track and rises through the
densely packed conifers. Follow this up
to a ladder stile on the northern perimeter of
the plantation.

Beyond the trees, a rough but obvious path strikes
out across open hillside, rising steeply over the sturdy
southern shoulder of **Hill of Strone**. The trail remains
clear, passing occasional grouse butts until the cairn

sitting at the heart of a broad summit plateau is reached.

With the glens of Prosen to the south and Clova to the north, Hill of Strone is well placed to offer **superb views** of both. The most striking features of the surrounding landscape are the corries of Loch Brandy and Loch Wharral to the north. The rounded summit of neighbouring Driesh, the next goal on this route, dominates the outlook to the west.

As the crow flies, the top of the Munro is less than 2km away. However, between the pair there lies a narrow col that must be crossed. The descent to the pass, which lies above Corrie of Farchal, is steep and careful navigation is required in bad visibility. While there is an obvious path down into the col, the route is less distinct on the upper slope of Hill of Strone.

From the base of the col, the path initially climbs steeply before the gradient eases off for the final approach to the summit of **Driesh**, where a sheltering circle of stones protects the trig point – and hillwalkers – from the elements.

Driesh is most commonly approached via the Kilbo Path from Glen Doll. As a result, there is a well-walked trail leading west from the summit. It descends over **Little Driesh** into a col lying just

Sheep cling to rock outcrops by the Kilbo Path

This is a great spot for views north down the valley to Glen Doll and south to Glen Prosen and the hills beyond.

below the highest point of the Kilbo Path. ◄ Climb from the col to join the **Kilbo Path** and turn left.

The origins of the **Kilbo Path** remain something of a mystery. Some believe it may have been an old drove road while there is evidence to suggest it was simply a particularly well-constructed stalkers' path.

The path leads west initially, crossing level ground dotted with boulders and rocky outcrops. It runs parallel with two fences, one low and one high, to reach a tall metal signpost originally erected by the Scottish Rights of Way and Access Society but now devoid of its arms.

Bear left, following the fence, and remain on the Kilbo Path as it descends south over **Shank of Drumwhallo**. Lower down there is another Scottish Rights of Way and Access Society signpost, this one intact, indicating the route of the Kilbo Path. Below it, the route enters a forest of pine and larch, the path dropping through a corridor in the dense trees to reach Prosen Water at the base of

the slope. To the left stands the ruin of **Kilbo**, a former stalkers' cottage.

Glen Prosen from the Kilbo Path

Cross Prosen Water by way of a metal girder slung over the lively stream and join a solid estate track on the other side. Here begins the long hike down the valley. Prosen is a long, lonely glen, eerily quiet in its upper reaches where the slopes are peppered with thousands of ghostly white tree stumps, the remnants of a felled plantation.

Beyond the bounds of this plantation, the track crosses Prosen Water by a substantial bridge and continues below wooded **Craig Tillelet** to a junction. Continue straight on at this point and the first occupied building in the glen appears in the form of a mid-19th-century white-washed lodge.

Old Craig Lodge is the principal house on the Glen Prosen Estate, one of five estates in the valley. Boasting diverse terrain from mountain summits, steep crags and corries, to open slopes of heather moor, riverside pasture and natural woodland, the estate covers 8357 acres. The main activities

Remote Old Craig Lodge enjoys a fine outlook over Prosen Water

include grouse shooting, fishing, deer stalking and farming.

The track runs alongside Prosen Water for a way before rising gently over rough pasture to pass an old corrugated iron shed. Beyond this it begins its descent towards farm sheds and a cottage at **Runtaleave**. Further estate buildings follow as the route crosses Burn of Farchal and rises briefly past the headkeeper's cottage to meet the public road just west of **Glenprosen Lodge**. Follow the road back past the lodge to complete the walk.

GLEN CLOVA

Loch Wharral (Walk 17)

WALK 12

Broad Cairn and Cairn Bannoch

Start/Finish	Car park (pay and display) at Glen Doll Ranger Base 5.5km northwest of Clova (NO 283 761)
Distance	25km (15½ miles)
Time	7hr
Height gain	1000m (3280ft)
Maps	OS 1:50,000 Landranger 44; OS 1:25,000 Explorer 388

This is a long and demanding route over two Munros located on the northern periphery of Angus.

Beginning with a lengthy track walk in, the bulk of the strenuous climbing is confined to the ascent of Broad Cairn, after which the gradients are shorter and less severe. There are established and well-walked tracks and paths for the majority of the route although careful navigation is required over the exposed high ground when visibility is poor. This walk is best done on a clear day when, thanks to its elevation, it offers superb mountain panoramas. Particularly rewarding are the views of neighbouring Lochnagar. Dogs should be kept under close control due to the presence of grazing sheep and ground-nesting birds.

The starting point for this walk (and Walks 13–16), the Glen Doll Ranger Base car park, lies at the end of the public road leading through Glen Clova from Kirriemuir. Head across the grassy bank separating the car park from the River South Esk, turn left and walk past riverside picnic tables to a yellow waymarker. Continue straight ahead, picking up a riverside path that initially runs alongside a fence. The route follows the South Esk upstream to a footbridge over the river.

Cross the bridge, pass a wooden bench on the other side and follow a path through conifers. It runs in a straight line to meet a track 300m from the bridge. Turn left, pass between tall gateposts and follow the track north. The route leaves the plantation and crosses open ground, passing over a bridge spanning the Moulzie Burn to reach **Moulzie**.

Just before the gate leading into Moulzie, bear right, still on the track, and the way continues north, running alongside a fence on the left. The track rises gently before descending to a junction where the main track swings left. Leave the track here and walk north, following a path that leads towards a plantation. The route does not enter the trees but instead curves left and runs along the western edge of the forest, wooden boardwalks crossing marshy ground.

The path meets up with the river once again and meanders along the bank to a wooden bridge spanning the water. Cross and rejoin the track on the other side.

The track swings right and then left, heading west up the valley and remaining close to the river. The gradient is initially gentle but after 2km, the route begins a more serious ascent towards Bachnagairn. To the right, the river, so benign lower down the valley, cascades through a series of waterfalls, rocky gorges and deep pools.

Underfoot, the terrain becomes increasingly rough until the track finally ends at a wooden bridge over a lively stream. On the other side of the bridge, a path enters woodland, climbing through a mix of larch and pine. Higher

The River South Esk negotiates a jumble of rocks below Bachnagairn

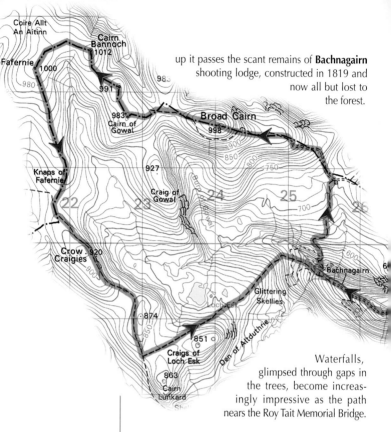

up it passes the scant remains of **Bachnagairn** shooting lodge, constructed in 1819 and now all but lost to the forest.

Waterfalls, glimpsed through gaps in the trees, become increasingly impressive as the path nears the Roy Tait Memorial Bridge.

Spanning a deep gorge, the **wooden crossing** is an excellent viewpoint offering a superb vista down the valley. Replacing an earlier rather rickety version, the bridge was constructed in 1984 as a memorial to Roy Tait who was killed in a climbing accident on Lochnagar three years earlier.

Across the bridge, the ascent continues, the path rising steeply to a boulder peppered with trees. To combat erosion, steps, stone paving and drainage gullies have been laid. Beyond the boulder, the path swings right. There are some boggy spots but generally the terrain is good and height is quickly gained. With elevation come views and there are some excellent ones down the valley.

After a long, unrelenting climb, the gradient finally eases and a well-constructed path crosses slopes of heather to reach a hut perched on the col. As it approaches the shed, the path skirts the edge of a fenced area of ground, arriving at a junction. Turn right here to access the hut, a wooden stable with corrugated iron roof built to shelter stalkers' ponies. ▸

At a junction by the hut, go left and a good hill path heads west to **Broad Cairn**. Initially the trail is well constructed, an orderly line of gravel and stone hemmed in by banks of peat and heather. However, as it rises over the hillside the way becomes increasingly unkempt, erosion taking its toll.

The rough line of soft peat pitted with stones emerges on to a flat section of shoulder where a wide highway leads to the base of a boulder field encircling the summit. While the path picks an obvious line through the jumbled blocks of granite, some rock hopping is required and careful footing is a must as there are plenty of loose stones waiting to snare the unwary.

The summit cairn sits atop a bulbous mound of granite. There are **excellent views** north to Lochnagar and east to Loch Muick. To the west the rocky apex of Cairn Bannoch can be clearly seen.

Turn left for a shortcut to the Broad Cairn hill path.

Carefully picking a course down through the rocks, descend the western flank of Broad Cairn, following a good path. Lower down, the scattered stones thin out and a pleasant tramp leads to the col below.

The path rises over **Cairn of Gowal** before descending into the col below **Cairn Bannoch**. From here it is an easy ascent on to the summit of the route's second Munro. Like Broad Cairn, the top of the mountain is flanked by stone – although not quite as much as its neighbour – and the cairn is perched on a slab of granite. Again, the views of Lochnagar are superb. There is also an extensive vista over the vast Caenlochan plateau.

Go west on an obvious path and where it forks, bear left, crossing a flat col with negligible ascent to a cairn on the summit of **Fafernie**. From here, the path, again obvious, descends south, crossing a broad slope of heather strewn with stone to **Knaps of Fafernie** where lines of rock resemble teeth.

In the col below Knaps of Fafernie, the path meets Jock's Road, although the line of the old right of way is fairly vague here. Occasional metal fence posts assist in the task of confirming its location. Follow Jock's Road up and over **Crow Craigies** and head south to a path junction in the col to the north of Cairn Lunkard. Turn left here and a reasonably distinct path rises over the col before descending towards **Loch Esk**.

As height is lost, the path improves considerably, offering a fine hike over open hillside with excellent views of Broad Cairn ahead. Entering larch woodland above **Bachnagairn**, the path descends to the Roy Tait Memorial Bridge. Retrace steps from here down the valley.

WALK 13
Tolmount and Tom Buidhe

Start/Finish	Car park (pay and display) at Glen Doll Ranger Base 5.5km northwest of Clova (NO 283 761)
Distance	20km (12½ miles)
Time	6hr
Height gain	920m (3020ft)
Maps	OS 1:50,000 Landranger 44; OS 1:25,000 Explorer 388

The Munros of Tolmount and Tom Buidhe are most frequently accessed from Glen Callater, in Aberdeenshire.

This route, from Glen Doll, uses Jock's Road (see Walk 28), a long established right of way, as its approach. Rounded summits on a vast upland plateau, the two are not difficult to climb but the long walk in, combined with the need for accurate navigation in poor visibility, makes this a challenging expedition. Beyond Jock's Road, paths are vague or non-existent and some sections of the walk are over open ground with no paths or tracks where areas of boggy ground will be encountered. Stunning mountain vistas and the opportunity to roam through wild upland terrain where wildlife-spotting opportunities abound offer ample reward. Dogs should be kept under close control due to the presence of grazing sheep and ground-nesting birds.

Leave the car park by its main entrance. Pass a forest walks sign and turn right, following a track up to **Acharn Farm**. At the next junction, by the farm, carry straight on, following a sign for 'Braemar via Jock's Road'. The track descends to a locked metal gate. Pass round the right-hand end of the gate and continue along the track, which passes below **Glendoll Lodge**, formerly a youth hostel and now a private house shrouded by woodland.

At the next junction, a short walk on, continue straight ahead, following signs for 'Coire Fee NNR'. The wide forest road follows the White Water upstream. Ignore two tracks coming in from the right, one just beyond Glendoll Lodge and the second below the impressive crags of **Craig Mellon**, and stay with the river.

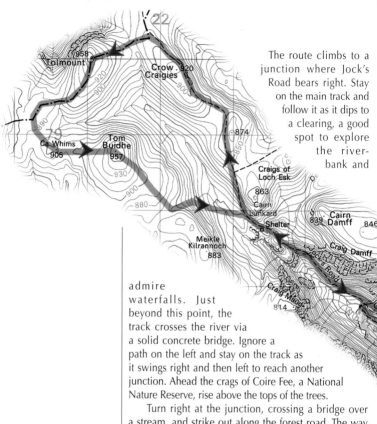

The route climbs to a junction where Jock's Road bears right. Stay on the main track and follow it as it dips to a clearing, a good spot to explore the river-bank and

admire waterfalls. Just beyond this point, the track crosses the river via a solid concrete bridge. Ignore a path on the left and stay on the track as it swings right and then left to reach another junction. Ahead the crags of Coire Fee, a National Nature Reserve, rise above the tops of the trees.

Turn right at the junction, crossing a bridge over a stream, and strike out along the forest road. The way leads through a plantation of Scots pine and larch, passing below huge boulders perched precariously above the track. At the top of a long incline the track ends and a path continues to the northern edge of the forest where a wooden footbridge spans the White Water. Ahead lies the wilder upper reaches of Glen Doll, a vast amphitheatre encircled by high cliffs and great bluffs of rock.

Cross the bridge and a narrow path running alongside a forest fence rises to meet Jock's Road at a way-marker post. Turn left and follow the long-established right of way up the valley. The route is well graded, gaining height steadily as it rises over the lower slopes of

Cairn Damff. Pause occasionally and look back down the valley for views over Glen Doll to the bulky mountain of Driesh.

Higher up the ascent is stiffer, the path snaking above a narrow waterfall and below rocky outcrops to reach Davy's Bourach (see Walk 28), a rough and ready mountain refuge built into the hillside (marked 'Shelter' on the OS map). The red metal door is easily spotted. ▸

Beyond Davy's Bourach, Jock's Road continues north. Due to the nature of the terrain, the path is less easy to follow and careful navigation is required. Crossing rough grass and frequent boggy patches of ground, it is easy to veer off course, particularly if visibility is not good. The path rises over the western flank of **Cairn Lunkard** and continues up and over an unnamed top 800m to the north. From here it dips briefly before mounting **Crow Craigies**, the top marked by a cairn lying amid scattered rock.

A short hike to a prominent cairn located on a mound to the south of the shelter is rewarded with excellent views down the glen.

On a clear day, **mountain vistas** unfold in all directions. In the far distance the high peaks of the Cairngorms dominate the skyline. Closer to home Carn an t-Sagairt Mòr, Cairn Bannoch, Broad Cairn and Lochnagar are particularly prominent, while both Tolmount and Tom Buidhe are visible to the west, Tolmount's stone-strewn summit an easily identifiable landmark.

Remaining on Jock's Road, descend for 500m before swinging southwest to reach the col below Tolmount. ▸

A path does cross from Knaps of Fafernie to Tolmount but it is fairly vague and easily missed.

95

There are bands of peaty bog and mossy marsh to negotiate in the col but long strides are sufficient to overcome both and a decent path rises up the eastern shoulder of the mountain. Higher up, it weaves through rocks, indication that the summit cairn is close at hand.

> Despite its rather benign appearance when approached from the south, **Tolmount** boasts an impressive array of crags and cliffs overhanging Glen Callater, to the north. Only a tiny glimpse of these mighty battlements can be enjoyed from the summit.

Descend southwest, passing the remains of a stone shelter lying just below the summit, and follow a good path that runs parallel with an old boundary fence, now little more than the occasional rusty metal post. Continue on this line to cross a shallow col and then contour round on to the top of **Ca Whims**. From here an undemanding

Tolmount from Jock's Road

climb leads east to the cairn atop the otherwise feature-less mound that is **Tom Buidhe**.

The dome of Tom Buidhe rises from a valley pitted with peat hags

The descent is largely pathless but has as its goal Davy's Bourach on Jock's Road. Head south down gently sloping hillside initially to a shallow col below Tom Buidhe then bear east, following a stream that descends to join the White Water in the base of the valley. There are plenty of spots where conveniently placed stones assist with crossing the water ahead of a short climb over open hillside to the howff.

Walk back down Jock's Road to **Glendoll Forest**. Enter the trees at a wooden gate beyond the waymarker post encountered earlier (above the bridge over White Water) and follow a good track through the trees. After 2km, the route meets the forest road taken at the outset of the walk. Turn left and follow this back to the car park at Glen Doll Ranger Base.

WALK 14
Driesh and Mayar

Start/Finish	Car park (pay and display) at Glen Doll Ranger Base 5.5km northwest of Clova (NO 283 761)
Distance	14km (8¾ miles)
Time	4hr 30min
Height gain	900m (2955ft)
Maps	OS 1:50,000 Landranger 44; OS 1:25,000 Explorer 388

Thanks to an uncomplicated ascent, generations of novice hillwalkers have started their Munro-bagging careers on the neighbouring peaks of Driesh and Mayar. The Kilbo Path offers a clear-cut if strenuous route up from Glen Doll, while the descent into craggy Corrie Fee provides a dramatic end to the day. There are easily followed tracks and paths throughout, but if visibility is poor good navigation skills are required over the high ground. Underfoot conditions are generally excellent with only a few boggy patches along the way. Dogs should be kept under close control due to the presence of grazing sheep, ground-nesting birds and the important conservation status of Corrie Fee.

Leave the car park by its main entrance and turn right, following a track that rises gently to **Acharn Farm**. At the junction by the farm carry straight on, following a Scottish Rights of Way and Access Society sign for 'Glen Prosen via the Kilbo Path'. The track descends to a locked gate. Pass through a gap at the right-hand end and continue along the track to the next junction.

Turn left, following a sign for 'Doll Walk' and, a little further on, pass a Kilbo Path marker post on the right. Beyond this, the track crosses a concrete bridge spanning the White Water.

At the next junction, stay on the main track, ignoring grassy paths that branch left and right. The track curves right and rises over a steady incline. Further up, beyond a hairpin bend, the Kilbo Path (signed) branches right and rises into the forest, accompanied by a small stream.

The ascent is arduous but there is brief respite further up when the path emerges from the trees on to a track.

Cross the track and the path continues over open hillside. Higher up the route re-enters woodland and then crosses Burn of Kilbo by stepping-stones. Beyond this point, it rises to the southern edge of **Glendoll Forest**.

The well-defined Kilbo Path climbs from here over the **Shank of Drumfollow**. It is a long but well-graded ascent and as height is gained vistas open out over Glendoll Forest to the hills and mountains beyond.

Nearing the highest point of the Kilbo Path, the way splits. Go left and a narrow path leads to an airy col where there are views south over Glen Prosen. Bear left across the col, heading in a southeasterly direction, and a path rises over **Little Driesh**. At this point the hard work is over. From Little Driesh walk east over a shallow col and enjoy an undemanding ascent to the top of **Driesh**. ▶

On the summit there is a trig point nestling in a circle of stones that provides shelter from the elements.

There are **great views** to savour. Mayar lies to the west while Broad Cairn and Lochnagar dominate the vista to the north. To the south the hills are lower but no less dramatic.

Return to the col below **Little Driesh** and head up to rejoin the Kilbo Path. Turn left and follow the old byway – a grassy track – as it runs parallel with a pair of fences on the right. The higher of the two fences soon peels off to the right. However, the lower, rather broken, fence line remains with the track until a metal signpost missing its arms is reached.

Leave the fence here and continue straight ahead, a good path leading west towards the well-defined summit of **Mayar**. The path of peat and stone roams over a flat, grassy plain. It dips to cross a mossy stream gully and then skirts by a peaty pool where soft ground is encountered. Beyond this the slope becomes steeper, the path rising over stony ground to Mayar's summit cairn. There are views west to Glas Maol and Creag Leacach from here.

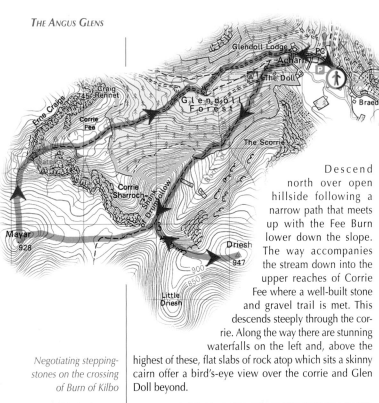

Descend north over open hillside following a narrow path that meets up with the Fee Burn lower down the slope. The way accompanies the stream down into the upper reaches of Corrie Fee where a well-built stone and gravel trail is met. This descends steeply through the corrie. Along the way there are stunning waterfalls on the left and, above the highest of these, flat slabs of rock atop which sits a skinny cairn offer a bird's-eye view over the corrie and Glen Doll beyond.

Negotiating stepping-stones on the crossing of Burn of Kilbo

100

CORRIE FEE

Described as an 'alpine amphitheatre' by Scottish Natural Heritage, Corrie Fee's stunning glacial scenery is a paradise for botanists, boasting an array of rare mountain plants. As such it is an important National Nature Reserve.

North-facing gullies give shelter to montane scrub species and damp crevices provide niches for the dainty alpine woodsia and oblong woodsia ferns, while outcrops of limestone and calcareous schists support arctic-alpine plants such as the nationally rare alpine gentian and alpine fleabane.

Steep unstable slopes along the base of the crag (out of reach of grazing animals) have a patchy distribution of alpine milk vetch, alpine saxifrage, rock speedwell and yellow oxytropis. Somewhat more abundant but still crag-bound are cushions of moss campion, purple saxifrage and the distinctive blue-green succulent roseroot. Melancholy thistle, common rockrose, northern bedstraw and fragrant orchid are frequently found on steep grassy slopes whilst, along rivulets, the tiny Scottish asphodel, frog orchid and early marsh orchid are less conspicuous and often go unseen.

The high crags are home to golden eagle, peregrine falcon and raven. Lower down, where the Fee Burn meanders through glacial moraine, efforts are being made to re-establish colonies of water vole, driven from the area by invading mink.

The path weaves through glacial moraine in Corrie Fee

Corrie Fee from Glendoll Forest

Below the slabs of rock, the path, lined with harebells and other wild flowers in late spring and summer, zigzags down beneath high cliffs and crags to the base of the corrie where it proceeds east, meandering over and around humps of glacial moraine. The path and the Fee Burn unite briefly, beyond which stone steps rise to the edge of **Glendoll Forest** from where there is an excellent view back up the corrie.

Continue on the path as it enters the forest and descends past a Corrie Fee National Nature Reserve information board to cross a stream by way of a large slab of rock. The path runs east from here through the trees, meeting up with the Fee Burn once again. A little further on the path joins a forest track at a wide turning circle. Continue straight ahead. ◄

Along the way, information posts highlight various features of the landscape.

Running parallel with the Fee Burn, the track descends to a junction. Go straight ahead, ignoring the route coming in from the left. The way sweeps right and then left to cross the White Water by a good bridge. Rising past the turn-off for Jock's Road on the left, the track leads straight back to Glen Doll Ranger Base.

WALK 15

Cairn Broadlands and Craig Mellon

Start/Finish	Car park (pay and display) at Glen Doll Ranger Base 5.5km northwest of Clova (NO 283 761)
Distance	15km (9½ miles)
Time	5hr
Height gain	760m (2495ft)
Maps	OS 1:50,000 Landranger 44; OS 1:25,000 Explorer 388

Access to Cairn Broadlands and Craig Mellon is by no means direct. Dense woodland and perilously steep flanks on the southern and eastern fronts call for a circuitous approach.

This route, which requires good navigational skills over high ground, follows the River South Esk upstream before advancing from the north via The Strone. A steep and pathless ascent over grassy and sometimes boggy ground leads to one top and then the other, followed by a well-graded, but again pathless, descent into Glen Doll, crossing rough terrain dotted with peat hags. The final leg follows Jock's Road, a long-established right of way, back to the car park. Dogs should be kept under close control due to the presence of grazing sheep and ground-nesting birds.

Head for picnic tables by the river just a few metres from the car park, turn left and walk over grass to a yellow waymarker. Continue straight on along a good riverside path that initially runs alongside a fence. The route follows the South Esk upstream, skirting along the fringes of woodland to reach a footbridge over the river.

Cross the bridge, pass a sculpted wooden bench and continue along a clear path that enters dense conifer trees and continues in a straight line to meet a track 300m from the bridge. Turn left and follow the track north. The route leaves the forest a short distance further on and crosses open ground, passing over a bridge spanning the Moulzie Burn to reach **Moulzie**, a cottage and cluster of outbuildings.

At the entrance gate to Moulzie, bear right, still on the track, and the way continues north, running alongside a fence. The route descends to a junction where the main track swings left to ford the river. Leave the track here and walk north, following a path that leads towards a plantation. The route does not enter the trees but instead curves left on its approach and runs along the western edge of the forest, wooden boardwalks keeping feet free of marsh. ◄

To the left, across the river, Cairn Broadlands is clearly visible, precipitous slopes rising to high ramparts of crags and cliffs.

The path meets up with the river once again and enjoys a gentle meander along the bank to reach a wooden bridge spanning the water. From here, there are excellent views south down the glen. Cross the bridge, rejoin the track on the other side and follow it up the valley for a further 300m as it curves round the rocky eastern flank of The Strone.

Turn left to ascend **The Strone** without the aid of a clear path. Staying to the left of an obvious stream gully, the ascent, in a southwest direction, is initially steep and unrelenting but, higher up, the gradient eases significantly and there is a bird's-eye view over the glen below.

The route continues up the northern shoulder of

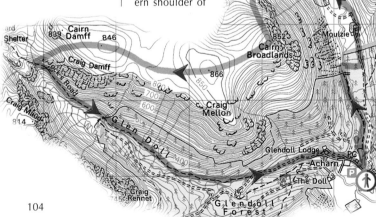

Cairn Broadlands, crossing grass and heather where there are marshy patches of ground. The upward slope bears south to reach the summit cairn. Cairn Broadlands offers uninterrupted vistas north to Lochnagar and northwest to Broad Cairn and Cairn Bannoch.

With no path as such, indistinct animal trails assist with the walk westsouthwest towards **Craig Mellon**. There is little fall or rise between the pair and it is a straightforward stroll, occasionally interrupted by darting mountain hare or grouse that erupt noisily from the heather. ▶

River South Esk below the craggy slopes of The Strone

From the prominent cairn atop Craig Mellon, it is worth venturing a little way down the eastern shoulder for an **aerial view** over Glendoll Lodge and down Glen Clova before beginning the trek to Cairn Damff.

Due to the featureless terrain, accurate navigation is essential here.

The pathless route continues westnorthwest towards Cairn Damff across rough ground, a wide expanse of grass and heather dotted with occasional peat hags. While it is tempting to stray close to the edge of the escarpment, if only to grab a glimpse of Glen Doll below, the going is easier on the plateau.

Rock-strewn Cairn Damff

From the 846m summit of **Cairn Damff** continue westsouthwest, descending a largely rock-free slope to meet Jock's Road. A fine mountain path with an air of rugged reliability, it descends slopes of rock-strewn heather above the cascading White Water to reach a wooden gate leading into **Glendoll Forest**. Although dominated by conifers, rowan, ash and silver birch add interest, and after 2km of pleasant woodland walking the path emerges on to a more substantial forest track. Turn left and follow the track east. The route remains parallel with the White Water and there are some spectacular stretches of wild water and falls on the right. Approaching **Glendoll Lodge**, concealed in mixed woodland to the left, the track reaches a junction. Continue straight ahead, passing below the lodge.

Built in the latter years of the 19th century as a **shooting lodge** by Lord Southesk, it was for decades a popular youth hostel. Today, having closed its doors to travellers in 2002, it is a private residence.

The way rises gently, passing through a gate and running on above farm and Forestry Commission buildings at **Acharn**. Go straight ahead, passing the entrance to Glendoll Lodge on the left, to return to Glen Doll Ranger Base.

WALK 16

Ferrowie and Lair of Aldararie

Start/Finish	Car park (pay and display) at Glen Doll Ranger Base 5.5km northwest of Clova (NO 283 761)
Distance	13km (8 miles)
Time	4hr
Height gain	730m (2395ft)
Maps	OS 1:50,000 Landranger 44; OS 1:25,000 Explorer 388

Ferrowie and Lair of Aldararie tend to be overlooked by visitors drawn to Glen Doll by the area's more popular Munros or waymarked trails. As a result, they offer a real escape from the crowds, a chance to wander across pathless ground where there is a real air of remoteness.

While the long-established Capel Mounth route provides a well-graded approach from the base of the valley, excellent navigation skills are required over the higher ground where the terrain is largely featureless. The walk concludes with a descent through Glendoll Forest where sections of the track are rutted and muddy. Dogs should be kept under close control due to the presence of grazing sheep and ground-nesting birds.

Begin at the eastern end of the car park where a path leads out on to the access road. Turn left and cross the River South Esk by the road bridge. Once over, go left, passing round a locked metal gate to join a solid track leading north up the valley. The track runs parallel with the river, crossing heathland bounded by forestry. Following a line of overhead cables, it skirts woodland and areas of felled plantation, veering away from the River South Esk to cross Cald Burn by a substantial bridge. Upstream, small waterfalls tumble through narrow gullies.

Immediately beyond the bridge, turn right on the signed 'Capel Mounth' trail. A grassy path rises into tall lodgepole pine trees, curving left almost at once. The way climbs gently, passing under the line of overhead cables and, further on, goes through an old metal gate. The path

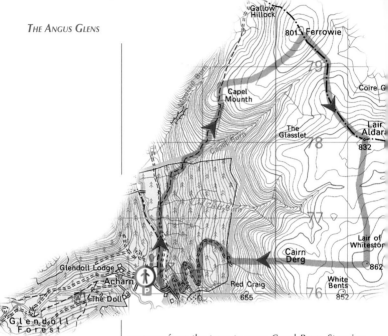

emerges from the trees to cross Capel Burn. Stepping-stones assist here and, with views extending north up the valley towards Bachnagairn and the mountaintops beyond, it is a good place to pause for a breather ahead of the more arduous climb that lies ahead.

Beyond the stream crossing, a series of well-engineered zigzags have stood the test of time and enable good height to be gained before the **Capel Mounth** leaves the bounds of the plantation at a gateway in a decrepit old fence.

Following the line of Capel Burn upstream, the path rises over heather moor, views across heavily wooded Glen Doll towards Driesh improving with every uphill step. Further up the steep southern spur of Ferrowie, the path veers left, moving away from the cleft of the stream, cutting diagonally across the slope before rounding the shoulder to reach the highest point on the Capel Mounth.

To the west, vistas up the valley of the River South Esk remain impressive. However, a whole new **panorama** now unfolds towards the mountains of Deeside, Lochnagar the most prominent.

Bid the Capel Mounth farewell at this point and head northeast towards the summit of Ferrowie. Pathless, the route crosses a patchwork of short heather, grass and moss, interspersed with the occasional swathe of black peat. Generally, the ground is solid and the slope is much more gradual. Higher up, the route cuts through a line of wooden grouse butts and, beyond this, the hillside flattens off briefly, crossing land dotted with pools and fairly sizeable tracts of firm peat. This is an area where red deer frequently congregate. Indeed, due to its relative remoteness, there are good deer-spotting opportunities throughout this upland section of the walk.

The level ground leads to the start of another incline, this one continuing right up to the summit. Aim for an obvious line of grouse butts running up the spur. Above the highest of these a well-established vehicle track cuts through the heather, leading to a slim pillar cairn and small stone windbreak on top of **Ferrowie**.

The route continues without the assistance of a path on to the summit of neighbouring **Lair of Aldararie**. While both sit on the line of the boundary between Angus and Aberdeenshire, there is no fence or wall to aid navigation. Descend southeast into the shallow col separating the pair, taking care to avoid narrow streams concealed by grass and, continuing on the same line, ascend the slope of heather and grass. The climb is not particularly taxing. It rises to an extensive and featureless flat plateau, the summit of Lair of Aldararie.

The next point on the route, **Lair of Whitestone**, lies due south. Drop into the col between the two and an easy ascent, again over heathery ground, leads to the stony summit. ▶ Descend west over **Cairn Derg** and then head down over a steeper grassy slope towards the eastern boundary of **Glendoll Forest** to meet a track.

Neighbouring White Bents offers a short optional detour.

109

The track enters the forest at a wooden ladder stile and gateway where a gate no longer hangs and descends through a dark corridor in the trees. Rutted and muddy underfoot, efforts have been made to shore the trail up using both metal wiring and tree branches.

Lower down, the route swings left and a more substantial track, albeit still rutted and muddy, embarks upon a long, straight and rather leisurely descent, passing a signed viewpoint where a gap in the pines affords a slender glimpse of the valley below. A less-constricted view of Glen Clova can be found at the next bend, where the track swings sharp right.

Beyond this hairpin, the route descends apace, looping down through the trees. Crossbills, siskins and jays are among the forest-dwelling birds that may be spotted here, sharing the sanctuary of the high branches with red squirrels.

The track emerges briefly from the heavy blanket of conifers at a final hairpin bend, re-entering airier mixed woodland. It drops in a straight line to a metal gate beyond which the track meets the public road. Turn right and walk briefly on tarmac to reach the bridge spanning the River South Esk crossed earlier in the walk. Head back over it to reach the car park and the end of the route.

River South Esk snaking through the green fields of Glen Clova

WALK 17
Ben Tirran

Start/Finish	Gate at southwest corner of Adielinn Plantation on B955 3km southeast of Clova (NO 352 715)
Distance	11km (6¾ miles)
Time	3hr 30min
Height gain	730m (2395ft)
Maps	OS 1:50,000 Landranger 44; OS 1:25,000 Explorer 388
Note	Limited roadside parking; do not block gate

Loch Wharral is one of two corrie lochans lying in the hills above Glen Clova (the other is neighbouring Loch Brandy). Above the sheltered pool sits Ben Tirran, the highest point on the exposed plateau between the glens of Clova and Esk.

Clearly delineated paths and tracks make for a straightforward if strenuous ascent of the Corbett. From there the route crosses open hillside, circling the headwall of the corrie before descending via Shank of Catstae. A final climb over the elegant crest of Rough Craig completes the route. Excellent navigational skills are required if visibility is poor on the high ground as there are no significant landmarks beyond the trig point on Ben Tirran. The terrain is very good, although some boggy spots will be encountered. Dogs should be kept under close control due to the presence of grazing sheep and ground-nesting birds.

Go through the gate and follow a grassy path that passes, on the right, an old stone livestock enclosure before hopping over a trickling stream. The way rises through swathes of bracken and over glacial mounds, running parallel with the western edge of **Adielinn Plantation**, coniferous woodland 3km southeast of Clova.

Crossing heather and grass as higher ground is reached, the terrain is generally firm although the route negotiates some reedy patches where conditions underfoot can be moist. The ascent is arduous and there is no let-up in the gradient until, close to the top end of the plantation, a post-and-wire fence running across the

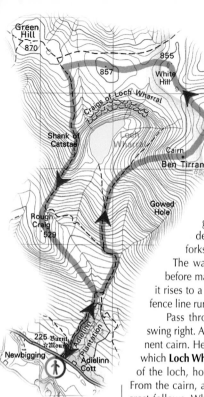

Green
Hill
870

857

855

White
Hill

Craigs of Loch Wharral

The Goet
△ 896

Shank of
Catstae

Loch
Wharral

Cairn

Ben Tirran
850

Gowed
Hole

Rough
Craig
529

225 Burnt
★Mount
Newbigging

Adielinn Plantation

Adielinn
Cott

Wharral is popular with anglers who fish the loch for brown trout; it also has a healthy population of pike.

path is encountered. Climb over this and continue to a stream crossing a little further on. The water is deep and fast flowing but stones assist in attaining the opposite bank from where an obvious path runs through the heather to meet a grassy track.

Once on the track, turn left. The way runs parallel with a stream gully, rising over open hillside at a less demanding gradient. Where the track forks, below a prominent boulder, go left. The way veers away from the stream gully before making a sharper left turn beyond which it rises to a set of wooden gateposts in a decrepit fence line running across the track.

Pass through the gateposts and immediately swing right. A grassy track climbs steeply to a prominent cairn. Here the craggy headwall of the corrie in which **Loch Wharral** lurks looms into view. The waters of the loch, however, remain concealed from view. From the cairn, a pleasant hike over a broad heathery crest follows. While the loch remains elusive, a sliver of white water snaking through a gully and down over rough rock can be seen across the corrie.

As the path begins to rise more steeply over the western flank of Ben Tirran, the loch finally reveals itself. Initially there is a tantalising glimpse of just the southern tip of the water. However, this quickly expands into a fine bird's-eye view, extending from the rough grassy pasture nestling below the cliffs right across the loch to its outflow. ◀

The path rises to a fork. Go right and follow a narrow but obvious trail. The route rises over a slope where mountain hare are a common sight to a **cairn** atop the southwest flank of the hill. The path flattens off and continues over level ground, a broad ridge leading to the

bottom of a short slope on top of which sits the **Ben Tirran** summit trig point, surrounded by a crescent of stone, a useful windbreaker.

The still waters of Loch Wharral lie below a cloudy Ben Tirran

> On a clear day, **views** extend west over the neighbouring corrie of Loch Brandy towards Glen Doll, east towards the hills encircling the upper reaches of Glen Moy and north over Glen Esk to Scotland's most easterly Munro, Mount Keen.

Walk from the trig point to a wooden stile spanning a double fence line close by. Do not cross but instead bear left, following parallel fences down the northwest slope of Ben Tirran to a small pond in the col below. From here it is an easy hike to the summit of **White Hill**, where there is a second tiny lochan. The fence line runs partway up the hill but veers right before the top is reached.

Descend west over open hillside without aid of a path to cross a shallow col and continue on to the neighbouring unnamed spot height (**857m**) lying midway between White Hill and Green Hill. Continue west over the next col and ascend partway up the southeast shoulder of **Green Hill** to meet a grassy stalkers' path. Turn left and follow this south down **Shank of Catstae**.

The path descends past a line of old stone grouse butts. To the west Corrie of Clova and the rocky glacial bowl containing Loch Brandy are visible, beyond which lie the mountains of Glen Doll.

Below the last of the stone grouse butts, the main path swings left. Continue straight ahead, following a narrow but clearly delineated trail through heather. The path dips into a mossy gully before rising gently on to **Rough Craig**. As the top of this low hill is approached, the path meets a rundown post-and-wire fence, by a scattering of boulders. Pass through the fence line and bear left, following the crest of the ridge.

Vehicle tracks through the heather assist over the top of Rough Craig while a more substantial track descends the ridge. The Loch Wharral corrie dominates the view to the north. Once again the loch itself is hidden behind a lip down which flow thin tails of white water.

Approaching the top of **Adielinn Plantation**, the track swings left, passing through a set of fence posts. Stay to the right of the fence at this point and follow it to rejoin the path ascended earlier in the day. Turn right and follow this down to meet the B955 at the gate by the southwest corner of the plantation.

Ben Tirran from the stream that flows down through Adielinn Plantation

WALK 18

Green Hill, Boustie Ley and Ben Reid

Start/Finish	Milton of Clova car park, Clova (NO 326 730)
Distance	11.5km (7¼ miles)
Time	4hr
Height gain	800m (2625ft)
Maps	OS 1:50,000 Landranger 44; OS 1:25,000 Explorer 388

Starting in the hamlet of Clova, this walk follows an excellent if steep path up to Loch Brandy, lying within a beautifully sculpted mountain corrie. It climbs above the glacial bowl to Green Hill before heading west. Skirting the upper fringes of a second corrie, it tops out on Boustie Ley where excellent mountain vistas await. Route-finding and terrain are relatively easy, with good paths and tracks for much of the way, although some movement on steep, rocky and pathless ground on the descent is required. Special care must be exercised when walking above the corries due to the presence of steep, unguarded drops. Dogs should be kept under close control due to the presence of grazing sheep and ground-nesting birds.

Leave the car park by its main entrance, turn right and walk briefly along the road, crossing a stone bridge spanning Corrie Burn to reach **Glen Clova Hotel**. Bear left to enter the hotel car park by a red telephone box and head up over the gravel, passing a whitewashed bunkhouse on the left. Continue straight ahead, the track passing a house on the right, to a Y-junction.

Bear right at the junction, following a sign reading 'Public Footpath to Glenesk'. A gravel path rises through silver birch trees, crossing a track servicing wooden chalets on the right. Further up, the path passes over a wooden footbridge spanning a small stream and squeezes through encroaching broom bushes to reach a metal kissing gate at the top of the birchwood.

Beyond the gate, the route strikes out across heather moor. The well-constructed path climbs steeply and with height quickly gained excellent views over Glen Clova and the hills of the south of the valley reward effort. ▶

Along the way stone steps assist over more onerous gradients.

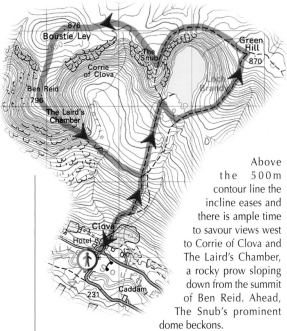

Above the 500m contour line the incline eases and there is ample time to savour views west to Corrie of Clova and The Laird's Chamber, a rocky prow sloping down from the summit of Ben Reid. Ahead, The Snub's prominent dome beckons.

A final short pull lifts the path on to the lip of the corrie cradling **Loch Brandy**, one of the best examples of a mountain corrie loch in Scotland. Unsullied by the hand of man, it remains in pristine condition.

Shaped like a foot, with its heel stamping deep into the rocky hillside and its toes tickling the heathery slopes beyond, **Loch Brandy** sits at an altitude of 638m and covers an area of 28ha. The shoreline extends to around 2.5km and while the water is low in nutrients and supports mainly brown trout and pike, the lochside and cliffs are home to rare mosses. Outlying pools are a haven for dragonflies.

Geologically, the most impressive aspect of the corrie is the great bluffs of grey rock that rise abruptly from the edge of the water and climb precipitously to the summit of The Snub. Scarred with narrow gullies of grass and scree they provide a spectacular backdrop.

On the lip of the corrie there is a junction of paths. Turn right and walk southeast, following a good path around the southern edge of the loch. The way undulates over low mounds sitting above small pools before curving left to negotiate the outflow of Loch Brandy. Well-placed stones ensure an easy crossing.

The path rises over a broad shoulder, the heather slopes to the left scattered with boulders. Less steep than the path ascending The Snub on the other side of the corrie, this route also affords the best views of Brandy's craggy glacial bowl. The incline is steeper higher up but eases ahead of arrival at the cairn sitting atop **Green Hill**. From the summit, Ben Tirran dominates the view to the east, while to the north Mount Keen is an easily distinguishable landmark.

Walk northwest from Green Hill, passing a second cairn. A grassy track leads round the top of the Loch Brandy corrie before dipping to cross a gully where a brief bit of bog must be negotiated ahead of the climb to the top of The Snub.

Evidence of the precarious geological nature of **mountain corries** is clear here. A substantial strip of the upper corrie wall has become detached and is slowly sliding away. In winter the formation of cornices of snow and ice put additional pressure on the fragile ground, increasing the risk of landslips.

A good walkers' path rising to The Snub and Loch Brandy offers an uncomplicated approach to this scenic spot

From the cairn on **The Snub** walk west, crossing a flat plateau of heather to reach the upper rim of **Corrie of Clova**. A narrow trail skirts round the top of the corrie, leading to vehicle tracks that continue in the right general direction. However, after crossing a small stream, bear left towards the edge of the corrie to avoid marshy ground and remain on the firmer high ground, heading east over grassy hillside to the top of **Boustie Ley**.

For such a wee hill, the summit, marked by a cairn, boasts an astounding **mountain panorama**. From Mount Keen, to the northeast, the view curves west taking in Lochnagar and the White Mounth, Broad Cairn, Mayar and Driesh with the lower hills of Cairn Broadlands and Craig Mellon also clearly visible.

Descend south over slopes of grass and heather on to the shapely shoulder lying between Corrie of Clova and Corrie of Bonhard and pick up a narrow but distinct path leading to a cairn marking the top of **Ben Reid**. While not quite rivalling Boustie Ley's all-encompassing vistas, Ben Reid nevertheless offers a superb view of Glen Doll.

Continue to the end of the spur and carefully descend the steep, boulder-strewn slope. A trouble-free line can be picked through the jumble of rocks without difficulty. Two-thirds of the way down, bear left to avoid larger outcrops and once on level terrain at the bottom of the prow walk east for an easy crossing of Corrie Burn below a small dam.

Continue straight ahead over moorland. A swathe of bare ground scattered with boulders offers one route while a peaty vehicle track runs parallel with this, to the left. Both converge upon the Clova to Loch Brandy path. Once on this, turn right and follow it down to **Clova**.

WALK 19

Dog Hillock, Finbracks and Manywee

Start/Finish	Road-end parking area by bridge over Burn of Glenmoye 6km north of Cortachy on minor road signed 'Glen Moy' (NO 402 646)
Distance	16km (10 miles)
Time	4hr 30min
Height gain	680m (2230ft)
Maps	OS 1:50,000 Landranger 44; OS 1:25,000 Explorer 389

The neighbouring peaks of Finbracks and Manywee are most easily accessed from Rottal Lodge in Glen Clova. However, this straight up-and-back-down route lacks any real interest.

This much more pleasant circular walk begins in Glen Moy and approaches via Dog Hillock, to the east. Easy-to-follow tracks take care of the main sections of ascent and descent while the upland portion entails a largely pathless hike over heather moor with some boggy terrain. Good navigation is required on the high ground, particularly in bad weather. Dogs should be kept under close control due to the presence of grazing sheep and cattle and ground-nesting birds. The route crosses a working grouse moor.

The start point for this walk lies at the north end of the Glen Moy road, a winding 6km single-track byway that leaves the B955 Glen Clova road at Cortachy. At the end of the road there is parking for at least half a dozen cars.

From the road end head north on a track, initially surfaced, that leads past **Glenmoy Farm House**, on the right, and continues around the edge of an adjacent farmyard. Ignore a track branching left into pine woodland and walk on past a corrugated iron shed to reach a metal gate beyond the cluster of agricultural buildings.

Go through the gate and follow the track over grassland to reach a second metal gate, adjacent to a wide arc in the meandering Burn of Glenmoye. Beyond the gate, the track leads north over rougher pasture, where sheep and cattle may be encountered, crossing a stream

The ruined cottage at Shank, a sad reminder of a lost community

by a wooden bridge adjacent to a derelict cottage. The track runs to the left of the cottage to reach another gate beyond which it rises over a reedy slope of grass to a ruined cottage at **Shank**.

> The cottage and a rundown stone barn behind it are the most tangible remains of an **old farmstead** that existed here. Close by there are the less-well-preserved remains of cottages, enclosures and rig-and-furrow cultivation, evidence that a small farming community once existed on the spur of Shank Hill. Aside from Glenmoy Farm, much of the agriculture has since disappeared. The land is now part of the 23,000-acre Glenogil Estate, which derives much of its income from grouse, partridge and pheasant shooting, fishing and self-catering accommodation lets.

A well-constructed stone grouse butt lying to the left of the track is a good place to pause and admire the view back down Glen Moy.

Remaining to the right of the ruined cottage and barn, follow a grassy track up the slope to meet a substantial gravel track. This track climbs steeply on to Shank Hill. ◀

Continuing to climb, albeit less steeply, the track passes to the right of the summit of **Rough Craig** and, lined with

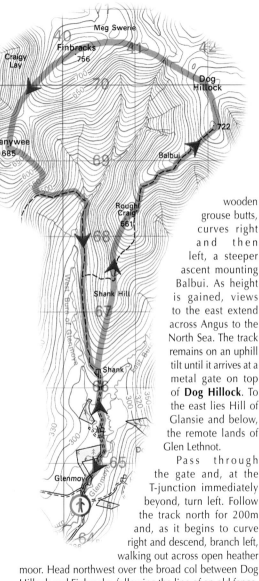

wooden grouse butts, curves right and then left, a steeper ascent mounting Balbui. As height is gained, views to the east extend across Angus to the North Sea. The track remains on an uphill tilt until it arrives at a metal gate on top of **Dog Hillock**. To the east lies Hill of Glansie and below, the remote lands of Glen Lethnot.

Pass through the gate and, at the T-junction immediately beyond, turn left. Follow the track north for 200m and, as it begins to curve right and descend, branch left, walking out across open heather moor. Head northwest over the broad col between Dog Hillock and Finbracks, following the line of an old fence.

On the way down into the base of the col, underfoot conditions are generally firm but there are patches of soft peat and soggy moss to negotiate. At the lowest point a wider peat hag must be crossed. However, as height is gained, the ground becomes firmer and an indistinct path, running parallel with the fence, comes into play. ◀ Continue up to a high wooden gate and a slightly shorter ladder stile in a fence that runs across the hillside. Cross the stile and stay with the fence line for the remainder of the ascent to the summit of **Finbracks**, marked by a rather stunted cairn.

Remaining on the fence line, descend the southwest shoulder of the hill into the col separating Finbracks and Manywee. Join an obvious track that leads directly to the top of **Manywee**, where there is a small cairn and a good view west over Glen Clova towards the mountains above Glen Doll.

Walk east from the summit to an electrified fence. Turn left and follow the fence line for 80m to a crossing point. Once through, head for a nearby rocky outcrop to pick up a rough track that descends southeast. This drops alongside a line of grouse butts before swinging right to meet another track at a T-junction.

Turn left and follow this down to cross West Burn of Glenmoye by a bridge in the base of the glen. Over the stream, the track rises to a wooden stalkers' hut. Although locked, the veranda along the front of the building affords some shelter in bad weather. It is a good spot for views up the valley to Finbracks and Manywee.

From the hut, a good track extends south, running parallel with West Burn of Glenmoye as it flows down the valley. Roaming across the lower slopes of Rough Craig, it reaches a junction below Shank Hill. Continue straight ahead to return to **Shank**, a little over 2km from the stalkers' hut. Retrace steps from Shank back to **Glenmoy Farm** to complete the walk.

GLEN LETHNOT

Burn of Drumcairn snakes through the valley
below Torr na Menach (Walk 22)

WALK 20

Hill of Glansie

Start/Finish	Car park at end of Glen Lethnot road, near Waterhead (NO 464 171)
Distance	13km (8 miles)
Time	4hr
Height gain	600m (1970ft)
Maps	OS 1:50,000 Landranger 44; OS 1:25,000 Explorer 388 and 389

This ascent of Hill of Glansie is a straightforward walk that begins at the end of the public road through Glen Lethnot. The route, which starts with a very steep ascent on to Hill of Berran, follows good tracks from Waterhead over the summit of Ruragh to Hill of Glansie beyond. The descent from here crosses some pathless terrain and sections where path lines are indistinct, particularly towards the end. Underfoot conditions are, on the whole, very good. Dogs should be kept under close control due to the presence of grazing sheep and ground-nesting birds. The walk crosses a working grouse moor.

The road ends 1km west of Hunthill Lodge, hub of activities on the Hunt Hill Estate. The estate stretches from the east of Lethnot right over the hills to Glen Clova and is primarily involved in deer stalking and grouse shooting.

Of the Angus glens, it is fair to say that **Glen Lethnot** is the least visited. The single-track road in does not actively encourage visitors. As it winds deeper into the valley it becomes increasingly less inviting. But despite the potholes, clunky cattle grids and wandering pheasants, the journey is worth making for it reveals an isolated landscape of rolling hills, grassy slopes and heather moor. Signs of life are few and far between and herein lies its charms.

Sitting by the Water of Saughs, the car park is informal and there is usually no shortage of space. Backtrack a short distance along the road and turn right, crossing a vehicle bridge over Water of Saughs. A good track rises through woodland, leading up past an estate cottage and a cluster of outbuildings at **Waterhead**. Pass through a metal gate and continue along the track, which runs parallel with a wall on the right and further woodland.

At a junction of tracks at the end of the wall, turn right and begin the strenuous ascent on to Hill of Berran. The track elevation is steep, an unrelenting climb over open hillside where regular stops to admire the view are a must.

> Remarkably the estate somehow manages to get its vehicles up here. Reward for effort is **aerial panoramas** over Glen Lethnot while, emerging on to the top of Hill of Berran, a magnificent vista of craggy Coire na Berran awaits.

On **Hill of Berran**, the track swings left and, now rather less demanding of legs and lungs, runs more-or-less on a level gradient, skirting along the top of the southern edge of corrie, to the

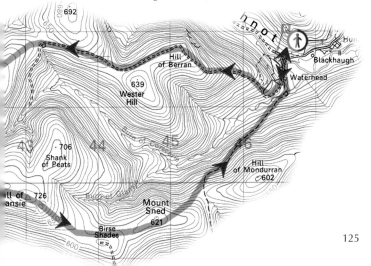

Water of Saughs and the steep track rising on to Hill of Berran

Designed to
accommodate
ponies on one side
of a dividing wall
and people on the
other, refuge from
the elements can be
found here.

right, and passing below the top of Wester Hill, lying to
the left. Beyond **Wester Hill**, the track curves right and
rises gently over the hillside, leading west to a stalkers'
hut at the top of Burn of Corscarie. ◄

Beyond the hut, the route forks. Go right at this
juncture and a gravel track rises on to the featureless,
smoothly rounded summit plateau of **Ruragh**. The track
continues down into the shallow col between Ruragh
and **Dog Hillock** where it swings left and gently rises over
a landscape of heathery slopes dotted with peat hags.
Grouse and red deer may be spotted here.

Stay on the track as it meets and runs parallel with a
double fence line on the right. Continue until a prominent cairn, lying between the fences, is neared. At this
point leave the track and walk over pathless ground, following the fence line on to the summit of **Hill of Glansie**.
The final stretch of ascent is undemanding.

The trig point lies on the other side of the fences
– one of them electrified – and a crossing point is provided. Pass through and cross a track to access the trig
point from where there are views south over Glen Isla

and the Vale of Strathmore beyond. On a clear day, the vista extends all the way to the east coast.

The track crossed to reach the trig point provides the most obvious means of onward passage towards the next significant point on the route, Mount Sned. However, between the two there lies an electrified fence with no safe crossing point. To avoid this obstacle, pass back through the fence crossing point on the summit of Hill of Glansie, turn right and follow the fence down over the heathery slope.

Descending the southeast shoulder of Mount Glansie, stay with the fence as it passes over **Birse Shades**. In the shallow col between Birse Shades and Mount Sned, the route meets an older, non-electrified fence running east. Follow this on to the summit of **Mount Sned**.

From the top, descend east over grassy slopes and banks of soft peat into the col between Mount Sned and **Hill of Mondurran** and aim for an obvious wooden stile located next to the end of a substantial track. ▶ Head from the stile across the track end and descend north and then northeast on an initially indistinct path that crosses the grassy northern slope of Hill of Mondurran. Careful navigation is required as the path is easily lost on the high ground. Care should also be taken when negotiating the ankle-twisting tussocks of grass.

As height is lost and grass gives way to heather, the line of the path improves considerably and is much easier to follow. It descends first to a wooden gate and then to a wooden bridge spanning the cascading Burn of Corscarie. Across the water, a short stretch of track rises over rough rabbit-infested ground to **Waterhead**. Turn right and follow the track down past the cottage and out-buildings and on to the car park.

Following the track from the stile to the summit of Hill of Mondurran offers an optional 1.2km there-and-back detour, with 60m of ascent.

WALK 21

Tamhilt and Hill of Mondurran

Start/Finish	Track end on Glen Lethnot road 1.5km north of Craigendowie (NO 513 706)
Distance	16.5km (10¼ miles)
Time	4hr 30min
Height gain	630m (2065ft)
Maps	OS 1:50,000 Landranger 44; OS 1:25,000 Explorer 389

This elevated circuit over the neighbouring hills of Tamhilt and Hill of Mondurran offers some of the best views of the remote upper reaches of Glen Lethnot as well as extensive vistas north towards Glen Esk and east to the coastal fringes of Angus and the North Sea beyond.

The bulk of the ascent is completed early on and good tracks ensure trouble-free navigation and unhindered walking for most of the way. There is a short stretch of moorland walking along indistinct trails at the mid-point and a brief strip of tarmac to tramp at the end. Dogs should be kept under close control due to the presence of grazing sheep and ground-nesting birds. The walk crosses a working grouse moor.

Parking on flat grass adjacent to the road is available at the start of the walk. Head west from here up a solid gravel track, passing under a line of overhead cables. The track rises steeply through a wide bend before continuing in a more-or-less straight line up over rough pasture. It passes a series of rundown stone enclosures and the ruins of stone buildings to reach a gate.

Beyond the gate, the track strikes out across heath moor, the dome of Craig Duchrey in

128

view directly ahead. Ignore a peaty track that branches right and higher up a series of zigzags followed by a long straight lift the route into the col between **Craig Duchrey** and Tamhilt. ▸

The track swings left in the col and, after a short spell of level walking, begins to climb again. It snakes up the eastern flank of Tamhilt before descending briefly, running alongside a fence, to a junction. Turn left and pass through an open gateway in the fence. The track doubles back on itself for a short way before setting a course west, passing over **Tamhilt**. At the next junction encountered, continue straight ahead.

The elevated highway offers a **stunning bird's-eye view** over Glen Lethnot, to the north. The pink edifice that is Hunthill Lodge is clearly visible in the valley below as is the Water of Saughs and, above it, the distinctive craggy bowl of Corrie na Berran. To the south the ancient twin hilltop forts of Brown and White Caterthun dominate the panorama.

Continue to the next junction, midway along the ridge. ▸ The route goes straight ahead at this point. Passing

A brief and pathless optional detour can be made to the cairn on top of Craig Duchrey, a good viewpoint over Glen Lethnot and Hill of Wirren.

A track branching left here leads to an open stalkers' hut where shelter may be found.

A rainbow brightens the view east from Hill of Mondurran

through a gap in a fence, the track curves right and momentarily descends ahead of the final stretch of ascent to the summit of **Hill of Mondurran**. Just below the top the track leads through a wooden gate and the prominent cairn marking the high point, located to the left and separated from the track by a fence, is just a short climb beyond. Hill of Glansie dominates the view to the west.

Return to the track and follow it down into the base of the col lying between Hill of Mondurran and **Mount Sned**. The track terminates here. Cross a wooden stile adjacent to the track end and walk south on an initially vague path that contours round the eastern slope of Mount Sned. Careful footing is required to avoid patches of squelching moss in the col. As it progresses, the route becomes more distinct. It curves gently right to reach a second wooden stile. Do not cross this. Instead bear left, following the adjacent fence across heather moor. Stay at least 10m from the fence to avoid peat bogs and small pools.

Around 500m from the stile, the route joins a good track. Ignoring a gate on the right, follow the track as it rises east on to **Hill of Garbet**. This is the last real climb of the day, and after reaching its high point the track saunters over a broad ridge to reach a junction. Along the way, pause occasionally for views back to Hill of Mondurran and Tamhilt.

Turn left and the track descends steeply, twisting down **Shank of Ducharr**. Beyond a small stream crossing, the knee-pounding gradient eases, the route swinging east. Ignore a track branching left that services a line of grouse butts and continue to the next junction.

Bear left at this point, descending into the base of the valley where the track fords another stream. It is a trouble-free crossing with useful stepping-stones. Passing through a gap in a fence, the track crosses a third stream, again just a small one, before making a beeline for **Nathro Lodge**, a shooting lodge sitting in the lee of Nathro Hill.

Beyond the lodge four **memorial stones** sit by the track. The first one encountered commemorates the extraordinarily long life of Peter Grant. Born in Dubrach, a hamlet near Braemar, in 1714, Grant was a Jacobite. He fought at the Battle of Culloden in 1745 where he was captured by government troops and taken to Carlisle. He subsequently escaped and found refuge in Glen Lethnot. At the age of 100, he was awarded a pension by King William IV of one guinea a week and became known as the king's 'oldest' enemy. Grant, who died at the age of 110, was laid to rest in Braemar Cemetery. The other three memorials mark the lives of local people, including a former shepherd at Nathro.

Memorial to Jacobite Peter Grant, the king's 'oldest' enemy, who found refuge in Glen Lethnot after the Battle of Culloden

Skirting the southern slope of Nathro Hill, the track descends to **Nathro Farm** from where it drops more steeply to cross Burn of Calletar by a bridge sitting amid a cluster of quaint holiday huts. The track rises to meet a surfaced lane. Turn right and follow this through **Craigendowie Farm** to join the main Glen Lethnot road beyond. Turn left and walk 1.5km along the single-track strip of asphalt to return to the start point. Traffic is generally very light.

WALK 22

Hill of Wirren and East Wirren

Start/Finish	Lethnot Primary School, Bridgend of Lethnot (NO 536 684)
Distance	14km (8¾ miles)
Time	4hr
Height gain	610m (2000ft)
Maps	OS 1:50,000 Landranger 44; OS 1:25,000 Explorer 389

Rising to the west of Glen Lethnot, Hill of Wirren, a Graham, and neighbouring East Wirren are the high points on this circuit that begins in Bridgend of Lethnot, a tiny hamlet consisting of a handful of houses, a school, community hall and telephone box.

The Shank of Ledmanie offers a well-graded approach from the south and while established tracks exist over much of the route, the high ground is largely pathless and the walk crosses rough terrain here, some of it boggy. Fence lines assist but careful navigation is required. Dogs should be kept under close control due to the presence of grazing sheep and ground-nesting birds. The walk crosses a working grouse moor.

Parking is available on the west side of the road, below Lethnot Primary School. Heading north, set off up a solid gravel track that begins on the left-hand side of the school grounds. The route swings left and then right, rising between fields of rough pasture. It curves left once again and climbs above a small plantation to enter an enclosed square flanked by five gates.

Turn left at this juncture, continuing along the main track. Hemmed in by fences on both sides and then a wall and fence, the route rises gently, following a line of overhead cables. The track passes an estate cottage and outbuildings at **Dikehead** and, approaching an agricultural shed on the hillside above, splits. Go right at this point and follow the track as it curves left round the hillside, passing through a wooden gate.

Beyond the gate, the route leads straight up the valley, passing a small artificial fishing pond lying on Burn of

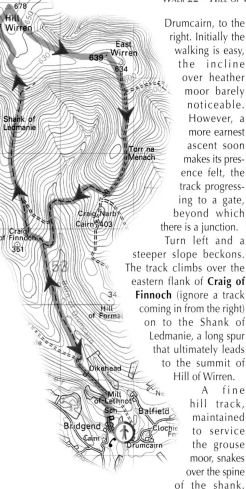

Drumcairn, to the right. Initially the walking is easy, the incline over heather moor barely noticeable. However, a more earnest ascent soon makes its presence felt, the track progressing to a gate, beyond which there is a junction.

Turn left and a steeper slope beckons. The track climbs over the eastern flank of **Craig of Finnoch** (ignore a track coming in from the right) on to the Shank of Ledmanie, a long spur that ultimately leads to the summit of Hill of Wirren.

A fine hill track, maintained to service the grouse moor, snakes over the spine of the shank.

Ignore a track coming in from the left and continue through a line of grouse butts. Above these shelters for shooters, another track branches left. Again, ignore this and stay on the main track, continuing up the **Shank of Ledmanie**. ▶

The elevated walkway affords excellent views west over Glen Lethnot to Craig Duchrey, Tamhilt and Hill of Mondurran.

The track ascending Shank of Ledmanie crosses an extensive grouse moor

Gaining height, the track curves right and briefly flattens off before tackling the next incline by way of a set of zigzags. At the top of these there is a junction. Turn left here and a rougher track strikes northwest. Passing below a wooden gate on the slope above, the route rises to meet a fence. Although the track appears to peter out at this point, it does in fact continue. Bear left and follow it along the fence line to a wooden gate. Go through the gate and stay with the fence, crossing a heathery slope to meet a high fence.

Turn right and follow the high fence up to a gate, located just above a wooden ladder stile. Pass through the gate and, keeping the fence to the left, head up over open hillside to reach the summit of **Hill of Wirren**. The trig point lies across the fence and can be accessed by following the fence to its top corner, a few metres further on. Bear left and cross where the wires are down.

Descend south to meet a fence and, bearing left, follow this down into the col. The slope of heather and grass soon deteriorates into a coarse landscape pitted with peat hags. On the whole, however, they are not too difficult to negotiate and decent corridors exist between the heathery overhangs.

> Along the way, occasional pieces of **plane wreckage** are encountered. These are the scattered remains of an RAF B-24 Liberator bomber. On 17 October 1944, flying in low cloud from RAF Leuchars, in Fife, to Cape Wrath, in Sutherland, it failed to clear the hill and burst into flames on impact. Miraculously four of the 11-man crew survived. Two years earlier, on 8 March 1942, another plane, an RAF Bristol Beaufort, also from RAF Leuchars, hit Hill of Wirren. It crashed into the hillside west of the summit and the crew of two died.

The fence curves left to reach the base of the col, where there are two adjacent gates. Walk past these, crossing a track, and begin the undemanding climb to the top of **East Wirren**, remaining on the fence line. On the summit, a track is joined. Bear right and follow this towards the trig point, which sits slightly below the actual

East Wirren from a moorland pool close to the top of Hill of Wirren

Stalkers' hut below Torr na Menach

high point. Just before the trig point is reached, the track arrives at a crossroads. Turn right here and pass through a wooden gate.

A good track descends south for 400m to a junction. Continue straight ahead at this point and the route drops over the eastern flank of **Torr na Menach** where there are views east to Montrose Basin and the North Sea beyond.

Ignore a heathery track branching right and remain on the main track as it curves gently round the slope to reach a locked stalkers' hut just beyond a line of grouse butts that cuts across the track. At the junction immediately below the hut, turn right. A track winds down into the base of the valley, offering a look back at the hills just climbed, where it crosses Burn of Drumcairn at a shallow, easily negotiated, ford.

A short but steep climb lifts the track out of the stream gully from where it contours round the hillside to meet the junction above the gate encountered earlier in the route. Turn left and retrace steps down the valley to **Bridgend of Lethnot**.

GLEN ESK

The unmistakable dome of Mount Keen (Walk 25) and
Glen Lee from Craig Maskeldie (Walk 26)

WALK 23
Mount Battock and Mount Een

Start/Finish	Small car park at BT phone box by Millden Lodge 6km east of Tarfside, Glen Esk (NO 540 789)
Distance	16km (10 miles)
Time	5hr
Height gain	730m (2395ft)
Maps	OS 1:50,000 Landranger 44; OS 1:25,000 Explorer 395

Mount Battock is the most easterly of the Corbetts and one of the high points on the vast Mounth plateau, topped only by Mount Keen and its cluster of outlying tops.

This long circuit, with some gloriously elevated sections, follows good tracks for most of the way. These, combined with distinct walkers' paths over the top, offer excellent terrain and make for easy navigation, although care is required on the exposed summit if visibility is poor. Dogs should be kept under close control due to the presence of grazing sheep and ground-nesting birds. The walk crosses a working grouse moor.

Set off up the narrow lane to Mill of Aucheen. The surfaced road rises through woodland, passing a former watermill, now a private dwelling. Above this, the road climbs below a band of pinewood to **Mill of Aucheen**, a house with assorted outbuildings.

Beyond a large green corrugated iron shed on the left, and sheltered by a stand of tall Scots pines, there is a junction. Turn right and a gravel track leads to Muir Cottage. Bear right in front of the cottage, head through a metal gate and continue over rough grassland towards Scots pines. As the track approaches the trees it curves left, and descends to cross Hazel Burn. Either ford the narrow watercourse or use the wooden footbridge located a few metres downstream.

The track climbs away from the burn and crosses open ground to reach a junction 1km further on. Turn right and descend to cross Burn of Turret. Climb to a junction a

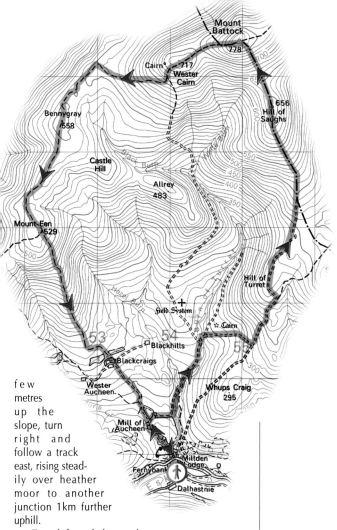

few
metres
up the
slope, turn
right and
follow a track
east, rising stead-
ily over heather
moor to another
junction 1km further
uphill.

   Turn left and the track
rises on to **Hill of Turret**. It continues to climb, steeply
in places, to the top of **Hill of Saughs**. ▶ Stay on the
main track, ignoring a track branching left. To the north
of the summit the track ends and a path continues straight

There are excellent
views east towards
Clachnaben and Glen
Dye below.

139

Mount Battock and Hill of Saughs

ahead. It descends to cross an electric fence, where the wires must be carefully opened using the plastic handles provided. Beyond the fence, the route negotiates a series of peat hags in the col between Hill of Saughs and Mount Battock. Underfoot, the ground is wet and muddy although there is a distinct route through that avoids the worst of the clag.

As the path climbs out of the hags and crosses a fence, another fence running at right angles up the slope provides a useful navigational aid. The ground remains boggy until a more obvious path reveals itself further up. Follow this and the fence to the top of **Mount Battock**.

The summit boasts a shelter cairn, trig point and panoramic views. Mount Keen dominates the skyline to the west while **Clachnaben** remains visible to the east. Crowned with a prominent granite tor, the latter is something of a landmark peak. As an **alternative outing**, it can be combined with an ascent of Mount Battock, starting near Glendye Lodge, on the Cairn o'Mount road in the neighbouring county of Aberdeenshire, and returning via Hill of Saughs and Glen Dye.

Glen Esk from Blackcraigs on the lower slopes of Mount Een

Descend west, following a fence on the left down to a wooden gate. Leave the fence at this point and continue west, following a faint track across the col and on to Wester Cairn. Stay with the peaty track, now more obvious, as it curves left and descends to meet a more substantial one on the southwest slope of **Wester Cairn**.

At the junction turn right and follow what is a solid highway of gravel and grit west. This elevated walkway, which affords excellent views both north and south, swings left and descends into a col. An easy stroll leads from the shallow pass on to and over the top of **Bennygray**, a rather insignificant lump on the ridge. Running above Glen Tennat, to the west, the track coasts down the southern flank of Bennygray before climbing with the minimum of effort required on to **Mount Een**. While the track crosses slightly below the actual summit, the detour over rough heather required to claim the top is short. The gentle ridge ramble ends abruptly here. The track drops with gusto, descending steeply and with little remorse over a slope dotted with grouse butts towards Glen Esk below. ▶

The views over the valley from this section of the walk are excellent.

Grouse shooting is vital to the economy of Glen Esk, which has some of the finest grouse moors in Scotland. The land over which this route crosses forms part of the 20,000-acre **Millden Estate**. It is regarded as a classic Scottish sporting estate offering driven grouse, pheasant and partridge shooting as well as salmon and sea-trout fishing on the River North Esk and River Dee. Millden has eight different grouse-shooting beats and 70 different lines of butts, all linked by a network of upland tracks. Estate activities are co-ordinated from Millden Lodge, a substantial granite-built 19th-century shooting lodge located close to the start point.

At the bottom of the grouse moor, the track passes through a metal gate and descends between small plantations of pine to a hill farm at **Blackcraigs**. Ignore the track on the right leading into the steading and continue south over rough pasture where sheep graze.

As the gradient eases, the track passes a signed walkers' path branching right to Tarfside. Stay on the track and, a little further on, it crosses a stream by a bridge and enters an airy woodland of tall Scots pines. At the next junction, continue straight ahead to reach **Mill of Aucheen** and retrace steps from this point back to the start.

Wester Cairn and Mount Battock from Blackcraigs

WALK 24

Hill of Cat and Hill of Gairney

Start/Finish	Car park, Tarfside, Glen Esk (NO 492 797)
Distance	25km (15½ miles)
Time	7hr
Height gain	1010m (3315ft)
Maps	OS 1:50,000 Landranger 44; OS 1:25,000 Explorer 395

This lengthy circular walk begins with a long and arduous ascent of the Firmounth Road, a right of way linking the hamlet of Tarfside with the village of Dinnet in Deeside. From the top of the old road, the county boundary is followed over Hill of Cat and neighbouring Cock Cairn and Hill of Gairney. The descent makes good use of tracks laid to serve numerous lines of grouse butts. In poor visibility, basic navigation skills are required on the high ground, although fence lines offer an additional aid. There are peat hags to negotiate in upland cols while a river crossing must be made on the return leg. Dogs should be kept under close control due to the presence of grazing sheep and ground-nesting birds. The walk crosses a working grouse moor.

Leave the car park by its main entrance, turn left and follow the road west for 100m. Prior to the road crossing Water of Tarf, turn right on a track signed for the Firmounth and Fungle roads.

The track climbs briefly through woodland. Beyond the trees it flattens off and strikes north, passing, on the left, a former Royal Observation Corps bunker. Only the top of the access shaft and an air vent are visible and the underground unit is securely sealed.

During the Cold War a vast network of these **observation posts** was constructed and most remain hidden in the landscape. Their role was to monitor fallout in the event of a nuclear strike. They were never needed and were decommissioned in 1991.

Map continues on
page 146

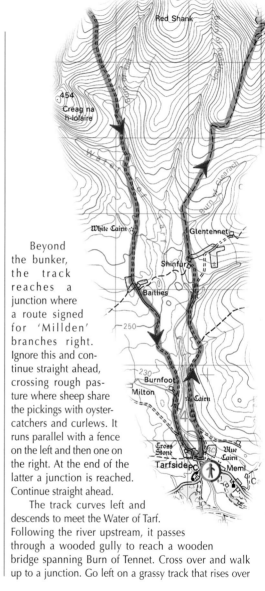

Beyond the bunker, the track reaches a junction where a route signed for 'Millden' branches right. Ignore this and continue straight ahead, crossing rough pasture where sheep share the pickings with oyster-catchers and curlews. It runs parallel with a fence on the left and then one on the right. At the end of the latter a junction is reached. Continue straight ahead.

The track curves left and descends to meet the Water of Tarf. Following the river upstream, it passes through a wooded gully to reach a wooden bridge spanning Burn of Tennet. Cross over and walk up to a junction. Go left on a grassy track that rises over

grazing land to a lodge and outbuilding at **Shinfur**. The track passes between the outbuilding and lodge and then curves gently right. Pass under a power line and continue over rough pasture to a metal gate. Go through the gate and walk north on a more substantial track crossing heather moor.

Water of Tarf running through a leafy avenue of silver birch trees below Shinfur

The track fords Burn of Clearach but just prior to the crossing, on the left, a small plank bridge offers a dry way over. Above this point another gate is encountered, beyond which there is a junction. Go straight ahead here.

The track rises over the southern shoulder of Tampie.
▶ Just below the 400m contour line a crossroads is reached. Continue straight ahead and ignore a track branching left a little further on. Beyond this second junction, the route swings right, contouring round the hillside ahead of the final pull up to the junction of the Firmounth and Fungle roads.

It is a long and steady ascent but as height is gained excellent views open out over Glen Esk to the south.

Four sturdy stone cairns line the approach while the intersection itself is marked by a signpost indicating the onward courses of both old roads. Turn left and follow the Firmounth Road as it rises steeply on to the summit of **Tampie**, passing through a high metal gate just below the top. ▶

From this elevated vantage point there are excellent views east to Mount Battock and west to Hill of Cat.

145

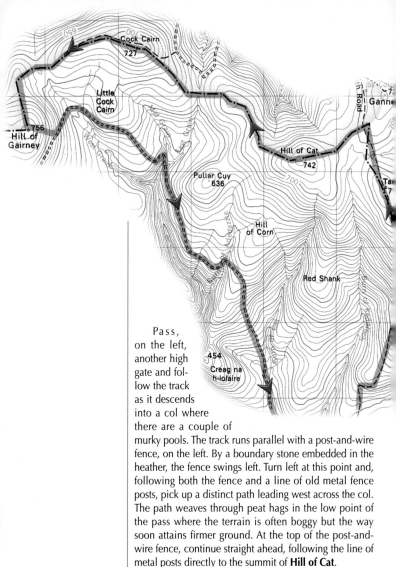

Pass, on the left, another high gate and follow the track as it descends into a col where there are a couple of murky pools. The track runs parallel with a post-and-wire fence, on the left. By a boundary stone embedded in the heather, the fence swings left. Turn left at this point and, following both the fence and a line of old metal fence posts, pick up a distinct path leading west across the col. The path weaves through peat hags in the low point of the pass where the terrain is often boggy but the way soon attains firmer ground. At the top of the post-and-wire fence, continue straight ahead, following the line of metal posts directly to the summit of **Hill of Cat**.

Staying with the fence line, descend the northwest shoulder of the hill, walking over springy heather, to the col at the top of the East Grain Burn. From here, a straightforward ascent leads on to **Cock Cairn**. The final top of the day, **Hill of Gairney**, lies to the southwest and the boundary line fence remains faithful, descending to a small pond in the col below ahead of an easy climb to the summit.

Head southeast from the summit for 400m to join a track. Turn left and follow this north. The track descends to cross the West Grain Burn and contours round the southern slope of **Little Cock Cairn** before dropping in the valley below. It is a lengthy hike down the glen, skirting round the western flanks of **Pullar Cuy** and **Hill of Corn**, but the route offers plenty of good views of the hills just climbed and the walking is downhill for much of the way.

After crossing Burn of Adedazzle, the track passes through a metal gate beyond which there is a junction. Continue straight ahead, a solid track of gravel and grit descending steeply to the crumbling remnants of a long-abandoned farming settlement, sitting above a swathe of green grass. Below the ruins, branch right on to an older track that swings right and then left before continuing the journey south to meet Water of Tarf. The river must be crossed. The ford is wide with few stepping-stones so head upstream for 20–30m to find better options.

The route rises briefly before descending to **Baillies**. Approaching the farm, the track runs between fenced plantations before passing through a copse of established mixed woodland. Bear left, passing the farmhouse to reach a metal gate. Beyond the gate, the track crosses two fields of pasture before roaming across heathland to a cottage at **Burnfoot**.

Passing an area of grassland on the left, continue straight ahead, dipping to cross a bridge over Burn of Calanach. The track leads through silver birch trees to a junction. Turn left and follow the minor road to St Drostan's Church, a simple yet elegant structure built in 1879. Beyond the church the road meets the main Glen Esk road. Walk straight on at the junction, crossing Water of Tarf, to return to the car park.

WALK 25
Mount Keen

Start/Finish	Invermark car park 6km west of Tarfside, Glen Esk (NO 447 803)
Distance	17km (10½ miles)
Time	4hr 45min
Height gain	720m (2360ft)
Maps	OS 1:50,000 Landranger 44; OS 1:25,000 Explorer 395

Mount Keen is Scotland's most easterly Munro, a solitary peak cut adrift from the rest of the big boys in the 3000ft-plus club by a quirk of geology.

Approaching from Invermark in Glen Esk, this route follows the Mounth Road on to the western shoulder of the mountain from where an excellent walkers' path completes the journey to the top. The return is by the same route. While Glen Mark offers a level approach that can be undertaken on a mountain bike if so desired, the climb out of the valley is steep and strenuous and the summit is exposed to the elements. Navigation is trouble-free in all but the worst winter conditions and the terrain is excellent throughout. Dogs should be kept under close control due to the presence of grazing sheep and ground-nesting birds.

Walk west along the road, crossing Burn of Branny and passing, on the right, Lochlee Parish Church. Prior to the road crossing River Mark, branch right on a track, following signs for Ballater by the Mounth, Queen's Well and Mount Keen.

The track leads to House of Mark, a former manse, below which the way forks. Bear left, following a sign for Mount Keen and Queen's Well and, beyond a metal gate a few metres on from the junction, the sturdy gravel track skirts the lower fringes of a band of Scots pines before striking out over heather moor dotted with scrubby silver birch trees. It passes through an antiquated metal gate and crosses a small stream before rising briefly, beyond which the way runs more or less level through Glen Mark. There is a wider stream crossing a little further on,

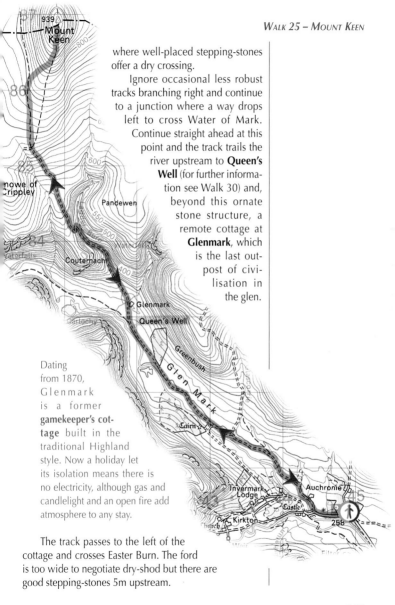

where well-placed stepping-stones offer a dry crossing.

Ignore occasional less robust tracks branching right and continue to a junction where a way drops left to cross Water of Mark. Continue straight ahead at this point and the track trails the river upstream to **Queen's Well** (for further information see Walk 30) and, beyond this ornate stone structure, a remote cottage at **Glenmark**, which is the last outpost of civilisation in the glen.

Dating from 1870, Glenmark is a former **gamekeeper's cottage** built in the traditional Highland style. Now a holiday let its isolation means there is no electricity, although gas and candlelight and an open fire add atmosphere to any stay.

The track passes to the left of the cottage and crosses Easter Burn. The ford is too wide to negotiate dry-shod but there are good stepping-stones 5m upstream.

The ascent of Mount Keen now begins in earnest. The track climbs gently at first to cross the lively Ladder Burn by a metal grid slung across the water. It follows the stream closely for a way, rising through a narrow cleft in the steep slopes that flank either side of the glen.

A long, concerted incline follows, a strenuous but well-graded ascent lifting the route away from the burn and gaining extra height by way of a pair of tight hairpin bends higher up the slope. ◀ Beyond the hairpins, the gradient eases but the protracted ascent continues, the track cutting a course through peaty heather moor. It passes a large cairn on the right, a good place to pause for a breather and admire the mountain.

Just south of the highest point on the Mounth Road another large cairn is reached, this one sitting a few metres to the left of the right of way. It marks the junction from which an excellent hill path leads directly to the top of Mount Keen.

Turn right and follow the path as it strikes east at an initially favourable gradient. A junction is soon encountered. Continue straight ahead and the incline quickly increases, the path weaving up through scattered rock, climbing occasional flights of stone steps as it makes its final summit approach. Before the top is reached, a prominent rectangular stone carved with the letter 'B' is passed. ◀

> **Ptarmigan** are frequently spotted on the top of Mount Keen. The bird's grey, black, brown and white summer plumage is perfect camouflage in this rough, stony terrain. A larger cousin of the more common red grouse, ptarmigan thrive in this Arctic-style landscape, breeding on mountain summits across the Highlands of Scotland. In winter, their feathers turn white enabling them to go largely undetected in the snow and ice.

Mount Keen's trig point sits atop a bulbous mound of granite, an easy scramble leading up to this exposed vantage point from where there are panoramic views. ◀

Mount Keen is now visible, its cone-shaped summit rising starkly from the vast largely featureless expanse of the Mounth plateau.

This is a boundary stone, marking the border between estates; they are common in the hills of Angus.

Below the trig point a simple stone shelter offers some protection from the elements; this is an exposed spot bereft of any natural shelter.

To the east, **Mount Battock** and neighbouring Clachnaben can be seen. To the northeast, on a clear day it is possible to see as far as Bennachie, a prominent little hill that, like Clachnaben, has a distinctive granite tor on its summit.

To the west, **Lochnagar** is the most easily identified mountain landmark while, to the north, the main Cairngorm plateau dominates the skyline. It is worth wandering out to a mound of rocks just north of the summit for a view over Glen Tanar, destination of the Mounth Road. The right of way can be clearly seen snaking down the valley towards Forest of Glen Tanar.

Mount Keen's isolation also makes it very difficult to incorporate the peak into any meaningful upland circuit. Therefore, the most practical way forward is to complete the walk by returning to Invermark by the route of ascent, via the Mounth Road and Glen Mark. After all the effort of the ascent, the long descent back down the valley, with magnificent views over Glen Esk, offers a very welcome change of pace.

Ladder Burn and Mount Keen beyond, viewed from the Mounth Road

WALK 26
Craig Maskeldie and Hunt Hill

Start/Finish	Invermark car park 6km west of Tarfside, Glen Esk (NO 447 803)
Distance	20km (12½ miles)
Time	6hr
Height gain	924m (3030ft)
Maps	OS 1:50,000 Landranger 44; OS 1:25,000 Explorer 395 and 388

Beyond the end of the Glen Esk road, rising above Loch Lee, Craig Maskeldie and Hunt Hill pair up for a fine hike in a remote corner of Angus. High cliffs and crags flank both, and while there is an excellent if steep track up the Shank of Inchgrundle and on to Craig Maskeldie, the ascent of Hunt Hill crosses rougher ground and follows narrower trails. Good navigation over open hillside is required from the top of the Shank onwards where paths are either indistinct or non-existent. The route returns via a good estate track through Glen Lee, calling at a little bothy on the way. Dogs should be kept under close control due to the presence of grazing sheep and ground-nesting birds.

Follow the road west from the car park, crossing the Burn of Branny and passing Lochlee Parish Church, which dates from 1803 and continues to hold occasional services. Stay with the road, ignoring a track on the right that leads into Glen Mark, and cross the River Mark.

The road curves right and ends just short of Gardener's Cottage. Bear left at a Royal Mail post box and a gravel track climbs through a metal gate to **Invermark Castle**. The stone tower dates from 1526 when it was built to guard the pass leading across the hills from Glen Esk to Deeside.

Over the years the structure has been altered and parts removed and what stands today is an **empty shell**. It is not possible to go inside the castle but a walk around the keep is every bit as appealing as there are plenty of interesting features to spot, including the main entrance which, to deter attackers, sits some way above the ground. A drawbridge that opened on to the roof of a long-demolished outbuilding accessed it.

Beyond the castle, the track descends and runs by the river. Light, airy woodland soon thins out completely and, as the route approaches Loch Lee, **Invermark Lodge** and a cluster of estate buildings can be seen up to the right. Continue on to the eastern end of the loch where there is a ruined church and a small cemetery.

St Drostan established a place of worship here in the early seventh century, although the current structure dates from the late 16th century. The graveyard is worth exploring; there are some fascinating headstones with macabre carvings, but the church is little more than a pair of gable walls.

Back on the track, continue west. The route passes through a gate next to a cattle grid and presses ahead

Shank of Inchgrundle descending towards Loch Lee, with Mount Battock dominating the skyline

There are excellent views up the loch towards rocky Craig Maskeldie and the Shank of Inchgrudle.

down the northern shore of Loch Lee, passing below a stone hut. ◄ Keep on to a junction near the derelict cottage at **Glenlee** and turn left. The route crosses the Water of Lee by a metal and concrete bridge and heads south to **Inchgrundle**. As the main track swings left, passing through a gate, continue straight ahead on a grassy track that rises towards an outbuilding before curving right. Below a sign for 'Glen Clova' (attached to a tree), cross a wooden footbridge spanning a lively stream.

A track twists and turns up through larch and Scots pine, emerging on to open hillside at the top of the airy woodland. Continue to climb over an open hillside of heather, bracken and grass. The ascent of **Shank of Inchgrundle** is long, strenuous but well graded and, as height is gained, there are excellent views east over Loch Lee. ◄

As higher ground is reached a brief detour right gives a dramatic vista over Carlochy, a corrie lochan lurking below the rocky flanks of Craig Maskeldie.

Continue up to the highest point of the track, on top of **Cairn Lick**, and then branch right, heading north over open hillside. Reasonably distinct vehicle tracks lead on to a well-defined walkers' path that descends gently into a col. There are some wet and mossy patches to negotiate but none is too expansive. The route rises on to a spot height at **683m**, where a cairn

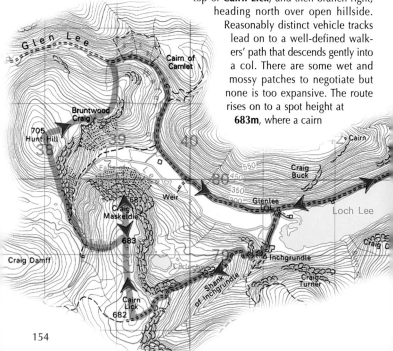

marks the top, before descending into a second col, this one occupied by a large area of exposed peat hag.

Cross the eastern side of this black ground and a none-too-demanding climb over more solid terrain leads to the cairn atop **Craig Maskeldie**.

> The exposed vantage point offers a **vista** over Glen Lee and Loch Lee far below. To the west, Hunt Hill can be seen while the view north is dominated by Mount Keen, clearly identifiable by the obvious path running over its southern flank.

Backtrack a short distance over the spot height top to the south of Craig Maskeldie and descend west, a narrow trail through grass and heather – wet in places – leading down to a wooden footbridge spanning Water of Unich, just above **Falls of Damff**. Across the water, climb briefly to meet a path and turn right, skirting round the eastern flank of **Craig Damff**. Follow this path for around 400m from the bridge, then bear left, heading into the col between Craig Damff and Hunt Hill.

Staying close to the rocky eastern face of the hill, climb north following deer tracks through the heather. A clearer path develops higher up but this stays close to the eastern face. When it reaches its high point, bear left and climb northwest over a heathery slope to reach the summit of **Hunt Hill**, marked by a small cairn.

Descend northeast following a fairly prominent ridgeline that runs along the top of **Bruntwood Craig**. There is no path over the slope of heather and grassy tussocks but navigation is straightforward. As the end of the ridge is neared, bear left and head down a

Johnny Gordon's Bothy in Glen Lee offers simple shelter in a remote spot

steep grassy slope, aiming for a bridge spanning the Water of Lee in the base of the valley. The bridge is basic – a single metal girder with a wire handrail – but it offers safe passage over the river. A heathery path on the other side leads up to a good track. Turn right and follow this east through the glen.

Around 300m from the crossing, the track passes Johnny Gordon's Bothy. For many years this tiny refuge was concealed within forestry but much of that has now been felled, making it impossible to miss.

> The **open bothy** is a simple, single-room stone structure with a wooden door and a tiny window offering a view on the world outside. Inside there is no furniture to speak of, other than a few tree-stump seats, but there is a stone grate where, for those staying overnight, a roaring fire instantly graces the place with a homely atmosphere.

The path on the right, which crosses the river by a wooden footbridge, leads up to Falls of Unich and, further upstream, Falls of Damff.

Beyond the bothy, the track curves right and heads south, remaining close to the river, which is dotted with small waterfalls and deep pools. Further down the glen, the flow enters a narrow rocky gorge at the end of which the track reaches a junction. ◂

Remain on the track and head southeast to derelict **Glenlee Cottage**. From here, retrace steps along the north side of **Loch Lee** to return to the car park.

MOUNTH ROADS

*Rising out of Glen Mark the Mounth Road runs
parallel to the Ladder Burn (Walk 30) for a while*

WALK 27
Capel Mounth

Start	Car park (pay and display) at Glen Doll Ranger Base 5.5km northwest of Clova (NO 283 761)
Finish	Spittal of Glenmuick, near Ballater (NO 307 850)
Distance	10km (6¼ miles)
Time	3hr
Height gain	540m (1770ft)
Maps	OS 1:50,000 Landranger 44; OS 1:25,000 Explorer 388
Access	Arrange pick-up at Spittal or walk 14km to Ballater for regular Stagecoach Bluebird bus service to Aberdeen; alternatively return on foot to start point via Loch Muick

The Capel Mounth is a route best tackled on a good day. While the track is distinct and easy to navigate, it crosses a high, exposed plateau. In fair conditions, excellent views abound. In bad weather the landscape can be very hostile, and during the winter the path is frequently obliterated by snow.

Setting off alongside the River South Esk, the route climbs steeply from the south, reaching its high point (690m) below Ferrowie. Once on the plateau, it remains above the 600m mark for a significant distance ahead of a final descent to Spittal of Glenmuick. Due to sheep grazing and the presence of ground-nesting birds, dogs should be kept under close control.

To combine this route with the Tolmounth (Walk 28, in reverse) walk from Spittal of Glenmuick to Ballater then travel by Stagecoach Bluebird bus to Braemar. From there walk 3km south on A93 to join the Tolmounth at Auchallater.

Leave the car park at its eastern end and follow a short path out to meet the access road. Turn left and cross the road bridge spanning the River South Esk. Turn left immediately, passing round a locked metal gate to join a good track leading north up the glen. Follow the river upstream, crossing open ground flanked by commercial forestry.

Skirting between densely packed rows of conifers and areas of felled plantation and new growth, the route

Map continues on
page 162

rises away from
the River South
Esk and crosses
one of its tribu-
taries, Cald
Burn, by a
bridge with
lattice
metal framework.
Once over the
bridge, turn right
on the signed Capel
Mounth path. A grassy
trail rises through the trees,
curving left. Initially, the
ascent is easy, the route passing below a line of overhead
cables and then going through
an old metal gate a little further
on.

Ahead, stepping-stones negotiate the lively Capel Burn before a
more strenuous climb is tackled, the
route gaining height through a series
of tight zigzagging bends. Above
these, the Capel Mounth leaves the
plantation at a gateway in an ageing post-
and-wire fence.

Running above the gully of Capel Burn, the path continues its ascent over heather moor. Higher up, it curves
left, leaving the Capel Burn behind. Cutting diagonally
across the slope, the track rounds the southern shoulder
of **Ferrowie** to reach its highest point. ▸

A wider, more rugged track strikes north, crossing
the western slope of Ferrowie as it descends into the
valley of the Moulzie Burn, down to the left. The route

Views across Glen
Doll and the craggy
peaks above the River
South Esk accompany
the initial climb;
Lochnagar and the
Cairngorm mountains
dominate the
landscape ahead.

The Capel Mounth begins its journey by the River South Esk in Glen Clova

loses height briefly before rising over the side of **Gallow Hillock** where the Capel Mounth leaves Angus and enters Aberdeenshire.

> The exact date of the **Capel Mounth**'s creation is uncertain, although early mapping confirms it was in existence in the mid-14th century. Despite its exposed elevation, it offered a convenient link between communities in Angus and those in Aberdeenshire and was well used by both cattle drovers and traders.

The next stretch of the route enjoys some of the best views. Across the deep trench occupied by Loch Muick, Lochnagar remains the focus of attention while the peaks of Broad Cairn and, behind it, Cairn Bannoch vie for the attention of the eye. Closer to home, the track undulates over rather barren topography, a moorland landscape devoid of any natural shelter or significant landmarks. It dips briefly beyond a junction where a track branches right, leading up on to Ferrowie. Rising from here over the western flank of **Black Hill**, another track departs from the main route, this one heading on to Black Hill itself.

Continuing north, the route levels off once again before beginning its descent to Spittal of Glenmuick. Slicing across the hillside above Loch Muick, it drops to a junction where there is a Capel Mounth sign, erected by the Scottish Rights of Way and Access Society. Turn right here for the **Spittal**, 500m further on.

Crossing the Capel Mounth's exposed high ground, a traverse best done in fair weather

In its day **Spittal of Glenmuick** was a welcome refuge for weary travellers. Established in the 15th century by the Bishop of Aberdeen, the once thriving township included an inn offering food, whisky and a bed for the night. There was also a chapel, and the name 'capel' – as in Capel Mounth – is thought to have derived from this.

Today the inn is long gone. The township was abandoned around 200 years ago but the Spittal remains a popular intersection for those heading into the hills. A small visitor centre, public toilets and car park sit adjacent to the ruins of the old settlement. Open daily throughout the year, the centre provides information on the local landscape and wildlife. A limited range of refreshments can be purchased here.

Onward route

From Spittal of Glenmuick, the public road to Ballater – 14km to the north – now follows the course of the old Mounth Road. While there is no public transport between Spittal of Glenmuick and Ballater, the Deeside town does have a regular bus service to Aberdeen.

Return route

For walkers seeking an alternative route back to Glen Doll, one option is to set off on the track along the south-eastern shoreline of Loch Muick.

Midway down the loch, it rises away from the water and climbs out of the valley, crossing the hillside above to reach a wooden stable (NO 256 808), above Corrie Chash. From here, a good path descends south to cross the River South Esk by the Roy Tait Memorial Bridge at Bachnagairn. A path and then track leads down the valley to Glen Doll Ranger Base.

Combined with the Capel Mounth route, this creates a 25km circuit with a total ascent of 980m that could be undertaken in around seven hours.

WALK 28
Tolmounth

Start	Car park (pay and display) at Glen Doll Ranger Base 5.5km northwest of Clova (NO 283 761)
Finish	Auchallater, 3km south of Braemar on A93 (NO 155 882)
Distance	20km (12½ miles)
Time	6hr
Height gain	770m (2525ft)
Maps	OS 1:50,000 Landranger 43 and 44; OS 1:25,000 Explorer 388
Access	Arrange pick-up at Auchallater or walk 3km north to Braemar for regular Stagecoach Bluebird bus service to Aberdeen; alternatively return on foot to start point

The Tolmounth – better known as Jock's Road – is the highest of the Mounth Roads, crossing a vast and largely featureless plateau on its course between Glen Doll and Braemar. For this reason alone it is a challenging expedition and one that is best attempted in good weather. During the winter, snow frequently covers the route and there is scant natural shelter from the elements on the high ground. Here too the path becomes indistinct and excellent navigational skills are required for a safe traverse, whatever the conditions. Refuge may be found at Callater Stables bothy and Davy's Bourach, below Cairn Lunkard. Due to sheep grazing and the presence of ground-nesting birds, dogs should be kept under close control.

To combine this route with the Capel Mounth (Walk 27, in reverse) walk 3km north to Braemar on A93 then travel by Stagecoach Bluebird bus to Ballater. From there walk 14km south on minor road to Spittal of Glenmuick to join Capel Mounth.

The route begins at the Glen Doll Ranger Base. Leave the car park by its main entrance, pass a forest walks sign and turn right, following a track up to **Acharn Farm**. At the next junction, by the farm, carry straight on, following a sign for 'Braemar via Jock's Road'. Erected by the Scottish Rights of Way and Access Society, it is part of an ongoing campaign to preserve historic routes.

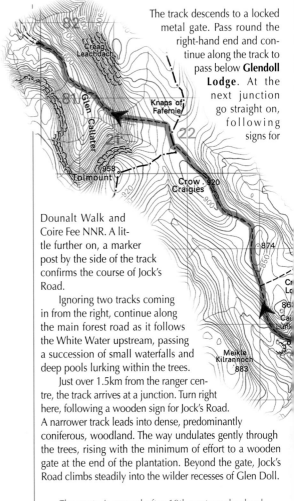

The track descends to a locked metal gate. Pass round the right-hand end and continue along the track to pass below **Glendoll Lodge**. At the next junction go straight on, following signs for

Dounalt Walk and Coire Fee NNR. A little further on, a marker post by the side of the track confirms the course of Jock's Road.

Ignoring two tracks coming in from the right, continue along the main forest road as it follows the White Water upstream, passing a succession of small waterfalls and deep pools lurking within the trees.

Just over 1.5km from the ranger centre, the track arrives at a junction. Turn right here, following a wooden sign for Jock's Road. A narrower track leads into dense, predominantly coniferous, woodland. The way undulates gently through the trees, rising with the minimum of effort to a wooden gate at the end of the plantation. Beyond the gate, Jock's Road climbs steadily into the wilder recesses of Glen Doll.

The route is named after 19th-century shepherd **Jock Winters**. Like generations of farmers before him, he regularly drove his flocks from Braemar over the Tolmounth to the market in Kirriemuir.

In the 1880s, however, Glen Doll landowner Duncan Macpherson attempted to close the route, denying the shepherds access. With the backing of the Scottish Rights of Way and Access Society, the case was contested and after lengthy legal wrangling in both the Courts of Session and, in 1887, the House of Lords, the shepherds were victorious, establishing the route as a right of way. It was a landmark ruling, setting a precedent that has protected public access to scores of other routes through the Scottish hills. ▸

Walking through Glendoll Forest on the Tolmounth

Aside from its legitimate travellers, cattle rustlers and whisky smugglers also used the Tolmounth.

Map continues on page 167

Squeezing up through the headwall cliffs and crags overshadowing Glen Doll, the path reaches Davy's Bourach. Above this tiny howff, the Tolmounth ascends the western slope of **Cairn Lunkard** and crosses a broad crest to attain its highest point, the summit of **Crow Craigies**. Here the way crosses an extensive, exposed and largely featureless plateau. To the north of Crow Craigies, the path becomes much less distinct, making this one of the most challenging sections of the route, particular in bad weather.

Passing between **Knaps of Fafernie** and **Tolmount**, the route swings west and begins its descent into Glen Callater. Dropping steeply, it cuts through the headwall

DAVY'S BOURACH

Lying below Cairn Lunkard, it was built in 1966 by Davy Glen, a man who spent many hours tramping the hills and valleys of Angus. Set into the slope, the stone, turf and corrugated iron howff is not the most salubrious of shelters, but offers a vital safe haven for those caught out on high ground by deteriorating weather conditions or misfortune.

Accessed by a red metal door, the refuge consists of a single room with a hard earth floor beneath a low ceiling. Its construction was prompted by the tragic deaths of five men – all experienced hillwalkers and members of Glasgow's Universal Hiking Club – in the winter of 1959. Setting off from Braemar Youth Hostel on the morning of 1 January, the party had attempted to traverse the Tolmounth.

Crossing the high ground – already blanketed with deep snow – they battled a fierce blizzard and plunging temperatures before succumbing to the elements. Rescue efforts were hampered by the weather and it was some weeks before all five bodies were recovered. Davy Glen tirelessly combed the slopes until all the victims were eventually found.

of the hanging valley and follows the Allt an Loch downstream to the southern end of **Loch Callater**. The path, which occasionally hops back and forth across the burn, is faint in places.

The Tolmounth continues along the northeast side of the water, a good path leading to **Lochcallater Lodge**, at the northern end of the loch. Here shelter can be found at **Callater Stables**, an open bothy maintained by the Mountain Bothies Association. ▶

It sits adjacent to the former shooting lodge, now used as a training base by Braemar Mountain Rescue Team.

A robust estate track strikes down the glen from the lodge and bothy, following the Callater Burn. At a junction 1.5km from Loch Callater, continue straight ahead, the track crossing flat ground to reach a bridge over the burn. Track and stream run parallel for the final leg of the journey to **Auchallater** where the route meets the A93 at a small car park by a road bridge spanning the Callater Burn.

Craggy slopes flanking Glen Doll and the Tolmounth above Glendoll Forest

Onward route

Purists seeking to follow the Tolmounth to its end in Braemar must endure a 3km tarmac tramp along the often-busy A93.

Return route

For walkers seeking an alternative route back to Glen Doll, terminate the Tolmounth hike at Lochcallater Lodge. A good path strikes northeast from here, rising above Loch Callater into a col below Creag an Loch. It continues up the western flank of Carn an t-Sagairt Mor. Leave the path as it begins to contour round the southern side of the hill and head directly for the summit of this Munro, following a fence line. Head south and then southeast over two further Munros, Cairn Bannoch and Broad Cairn, before descending to Bachnagairn. Walking parallel with the course of the River South Esk, follow a path that broadens into a track below the treeline west and then south to Glen Doll.

Combined with the Tolmounth route, this creates a 31km circuit with a total ascent of 1490m that could be undertaken in around nine hours. Bothy accommodation can be found midway at Callater Stables, adjacent to Lochcallater Lodge.

WALK 29

Firmounth

Start	Car park, Tarfside, Glen Esk (NO 492 797)
Finish	Braeloine Visitor Centre, Glen Tanar (NO 480 965)
Distance	18km (11¼ miles)
Time	5hr
Height gain	640m (2100ft)
Maps	OS 1:50,000 Landranger 44; OS 1:25,000 Explorer 395
Access	Arrange pick-up at Braelonie Visitor Centre or follow Firmounth Road 3km north to Dinnet for regular Stagecoach Bluebird bus service to Aberdeen

Crossing the hills between Tarfside, in Glen Esk, and Dinnet, in Aberdeenshire, the Firmounth is a long established right of way. However, much of the route in Angus has been upgraded to service grouse moors, the old trail replaced by a more robust track that lacks the character of the original. Rising to a height of 720m, the central section crosses exposed ground. Navigation, however, is straightforward. The walk concludes with a pleasant descent through pinewoods. Dogs should be kept under close control due to the presence of grazing sheep and ground-nesting birds. The route crosses working grouse moor.

Walk 29 can be linked with the Mounth Road (Walk 30, in reverse) to create a longer, two-day, circuit.

From the car park, where there are public toilets and an informal camping field, head out on to the main road, turn left and walk west for 100m towards the stone bridge spanning Water of Tarf. Just before the bridge is reached, branch right on a track signed for the Firmounth and Fungle roads. The two old routes follow the same course initially.

The Firmounth is believed to have been in existence as far back as the 13th century. Later it became an important drove road, used by farmers

169

in Deeside travelling with their cattle to markets in Laurencekirk, Crieff and Falkirk. In the 19th century agricultural workers from the northeast – many of them women – regularly made the crossing to work the harvest in Strathmore.

The track rises through a band of woodland, above which it levels off and heads north over grazing land. At the first junction encountered, ignore a rough track veering right (signed for Millden) and continue straight ahead, the route running parallel with a fence on the left. ◄

There are excellent views west over the Water of Tarf towards Hill of Rowan, a small conical peak with a tower – the Maule Monument – on the summit.

At the next junction encountered, bear left and the route descends into a narrow gully. It runs alongside Water of Tarf, silver birch trees sprouting from the riverbank, to a wooden bridge spanning Burn of Tennet, a tributary entering from the east. Cross the bridge and walk up to a junction of tracks where there is a Firmounth and Fungle sign. Following this sign, go left on a grassy track that rises over pasture to a lodge at **Shinfur**.

The hamlet of Tarfside has a handful of houses and a small school

The track runs between an outbuilding, on the left, and lodge and then curves gently right. Pass under a

power line and follow the track over rougher grazing land to a metal gate. Go through this and walk north on a more substantial track.

Map continues on page 172

Roaming over heather moor, the track fords Burn of Clearach. Just ahead of the crossing, down to the left, a small plank bridge offers a way over for walkers. Above the ford another gate is encountered. Beyond this there is a junction; continue straight ahead.

The track ascends the southern shoulder of Tampie. It is a long, strenuous incline. Approaching the 400m contour line, a crossroads is reached. Go straight on and ignore another track branching left. After this second junction, the route curves right, rising round the broad shoulder ahead of the final climb to a junction where the Firmounth and Fungle roads split. Four chunky stone cairns line the approach while, at the point of divergence, a signpost indicates the onward courses of the two routes. While the Firmounth crosses the hills to Dinnet, the Fungle heads north to Aboyne.

Turn left at the junction and the track rises steeply on to the

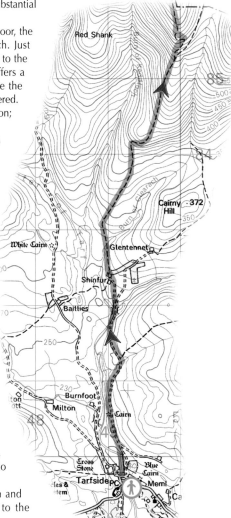

171

summit of **Tampie**, passing first through a line of stone grouse butts and then a high metal gate just below the top. To the east, Mount Battock and Clachnaben are the most distinctive landmarks.

Beyond the gate, the track gradient eases, the track passing, on the left, another high gate. Following the adjacent post–and-wire fence, continue straight ahead, the track dipping into a col occupied by dark peaty pools. An easy ascent lifts the route out of the pass and it continues to the end of the fence line where, embedded in the heather, there is a stubby boundary stone, inscribed with the letter 'B'. ◄ The Firmounth Road leads north, running alongside a line of high metal fence posts as it roams across the western side of **Gannoch**.

Walkers heading for the summit of Hill of Cat branch left here.

Map continues on page 174

On the right-hand side of the track, look out for **St Colm's Well** and a carved granite boulder bearing the words 'Well Beloved'. Dating from the 19th century, it was commissioned by Sir William Cuncliffe Brooks, MP and Laird of Glen Tanar.

Surveying Glen Esk from the Firmounth as it rises towards Tampie

Beyond the shallow col between Gannoch and neighbouring **Hill of St Colm**, the route dips briefly before rising gently over **Craigmahandle**. From here it is downhill all the way to the end.

Descending the northern slope of Craigmahandle, the route enters the tall Scots pines of **Forest of Glen Tanar**. The rare capercaillie and crossbills are among birds that inhabit the woodland while red squirrels and roe deer may also be sighted. After 1km of forest walking, a junction is reached. Turn right and follow the track down to a dam and bridge spanning Burn of Skinna. Beyond the bridge, the track swings left. Ignore a pair of tracks coming in from the right.

The route runs above Burn of Skinna for a way before it curves right, contouring round the slope to enter a

clearing at a junction. Continue straight ahead. The route runs above open ground, offering superb views up Glen Tanar. Further impressive vistas over the valley and its extensive pinewoods can be found at the track's next port of call, Knockie Viewpoint. From here, continue north on the track.

At a crossroads 600m beyond Knockie Viewpoint continue straight ahead. The track curves right to a junction. Turn left for **Braeloine Visitor Centre**, 600m further on along a good track.

Onward route

From Braeloine Visitor Centre the Firmounth Road continues north for 3km to Dinnet via Belorie and Burnside, following minor roads and farm tracks. The final short leg is on the B976 and B9158.

To link this route with the Mounth Road (Walk 30), descend a track branching left at Knockie Viewpoint to reach Knockie Bridge and cross Water of Tanar here.

Return route

Return to the start point by reversing the outward route. Alternatively follow Walk 30 in reverse from Braeloine Visitor Centre to Invermark car park and then walk 4.5km east on a signed track crossing farmland and moor to Tarfside.

WALK 30
Mounth

Start	Invermark car park 6km west of Tarfside, Glen Esk (NO 447 803)
Finish	Braeloine Visitor Centre, Glen Tanar (NO 480 965)
Distance	23km (14¼ miles)
Time	6hr
Height gain	620m (2035ft)
Maps	OS 1:50,000 Landranger 44; OS 1:25,000 Explorer 395
Access	Arrange pick-up at Braelonie Visitor Centre or follow Firmounth Road 3km north to Dinnet for regular Stagecoach Bluebird bus service to Aberdeen

Historically, the Mounth Road ran from Invermark, in Glen Esk, to Ballater, in Deeside. Over time, however, an additional spur through Glen Tanar connected the route to Aboyne; this walk utilises the latter. Following good hill and valley tracks where the terrain is excellent, navigating the Mounth is straightforward. Rising to a height of 770m on the western shoulder of Mount Keen, the route crosses high, exposed ground. Dogs should be kept under close control due to the presence of grazing sheep and ground-nesting birds.

Walk 30 can be linked with the Firmounth (Walk 29 in reverse) to create a longer two-day circuit.

Leave the car park at Invermark, turn right and walk west along the road, crossing Burn of Branny and passing Lochlee Parish Church. In 250m, branch right on a track, following signs for Ballater by the Mounth, Queen's Well and Mount Keen.

The track approaches House of Mark where the way forks. Go left here, following a sign for Mount Keen and Queen's Well and pass through a metal gate. The track runs below the garden of House of Mark and a strip of Scots pine trees before setting out across open heather moor. It passes through a high metal gate and crosses a tiny stream, rising briefly before running at a more or less

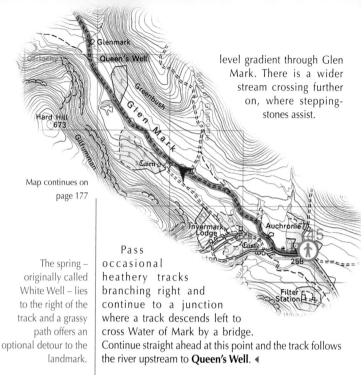

level gradient through Glen Mark. There is a wider stream crossing further on, where stepping-stones assist.

Map continues on page 177

The spring – originally called White Well – lies to the right of the track and a grassy path offers an optional detour to the landmark.

Pass occasional heathery tracks branching right and continue to a junction where a track descends left to cross Water of Mark by a bridge. Continue straight ahead at this point and the track follows the river upstream to **Queen's Well**. ◄

The slender granite arches of Queen's Well, constructed to mark a visit by Queen Victoria

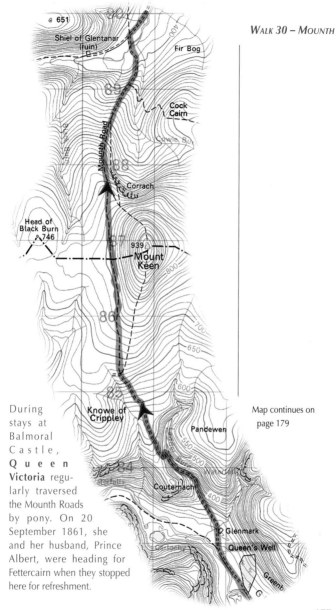

651

Shiel of Glentanar
(ruin)

Fir Bog

89

Cock
Cairn

Cowie Bu

Mounth Road

88

Corrach

Head of
Black Burn
746

87   939
Mount
Keen

800

86

700

650

85

600

Knowe of
Crippley

Pandewen

550 500

Map continues on
page 179

84

Waterfalls

400

Couternach

Barlochy

Glenmark

Queen's Well

Greenb

G

During
stays at
Balmoral
Castle,
**Queen
Victoria** regu-
larly traversed
the Mounth Roads
by pony. On 20
September 1861, she
and her husband, Prince
Albert, were heading for
Fettercairn when they stopped
here for refreshment.

The ornate structure was erected by Lord Dalhousie to commemorate the visit. Beneath stone arches, water gurgles up into a bowl that carries the inscription: 'Rest traveller, on this lonely green, and drink and pray for Scotland's Queen'. Later in the same year Prince Albert died, but Queen Victoria visited Glen Mark again in 1865 with her daughter Princess Helena. They lunched at the cottage at Glenmark before taking the water.

After crossing a patch of marshy ground to the north of the well, the grassy path rejoins the Mounth Road below the cottage at **Glenmark**. Passing to the left of this remote and lonely house, it fords Easter Burn. There are good stepping-stones a few metres upstream.

Rising gently at first, the track crosses the Ladder Burn by a metal grid slung across the water before climbing through a narrow glen flanked by steep slopes. A long incline follows, a strenuous but well-graded ascent lifting the route up from the base of the valley. It rises through a pair of tight hairpin bends on to the southern shoulder of Mount Keen.

While the gradient may ease the lengthy ascent continues, the track cutting a course through peaty heather moor. It passes a large cairn on the right and continues up to a second prominent cairn where a path leading to the summit of **Mount Keen** branches right.

Continue straight ahead, ignoring tracks leading left and right a few metres beyond the summit path junction. The Mounth Road crosses both the highest point on its route and the boundary between Angus and Aberdeenshire before beginning its descent into Glen Tanar. The track remains well defined, running down the crest of the northern shoulder of Mount Keen to cross a steel footbridge spanning Water of Tanar in the base of the valley.

Beyond the bridge it reaches a crossroads. ◄ Turn right and follow a good track running northeast down through Glen Tanar. After 1.3km, it crosses Water of Tanar by a bridge and then re-crosses the river after a further

The original course of the Mounth Road to Ballater strikes north from here while the track on the left leads to Shiel of Glentanar, a former shooting lodge.

Walkers on the Mounth Road, above Glenmark Cottage

1km. Bear right at the junction beyond this second bridge and stay on the main valley track to enter **Forest of Glen Tanar**, a remnant of the great Caledonian Forest that once covered vast tracts of Scotland.

A former drove road, the Court of Session declared the track through Glen Tanar a public right of way for all traffic except vehicles in 1931. Within the Scots pine trees, the track passes **Half Way Hut**, a little wooden shed offering shelter to walkers and cyclists. This is a good place to pause for a rest ahead of the remaining long hike down the glen.

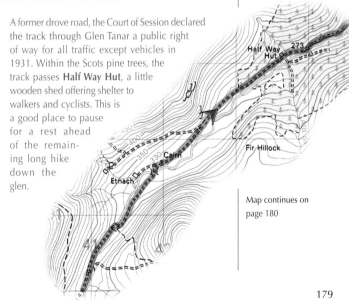

Map continues on page 180

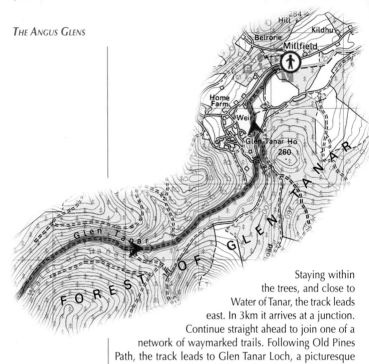

Staying within the trees, and close to Water of Tanar, the track leads east. In 3km it arrives at a junction. Continue straight ahead to join one of a network of waymarked trails. Following Old Pines Path, the track leads to Glen Tanar Loch, a picturesque tree-lined pool stocked with rainbow trout. The route curves left and runs along the eastern side of the water to a junction. Turn right here and cross Knockie Bridge.

At this juncture there are two alternative routes to **Braeloine Visitor Centre** and Bridge of Tanar, both following marked trails. The first, and most direct, is to turn left and continue on the Old Pines Path. Hugging the river, the track arcs right to reach a junction. Turn left here for the visitor centre.

The second option provides a link with the Firmounth (see Walk 29) and takes in Knockie Viewpoint, where there are excellent vistas up the heavily wooded glen. Turn right after crossing Knockie Bridge and, at the next junction, go left for the viewpoint. The Firmounth strikes south from here. To reach the visitor centre, follow the trail north. The route crosses another track before curving right to a junction. Turn left here for Braeloine.

Onward route
From Bridge of Tanar (via the Firmounth Road) continue north for 3km to Dinnet via Belorie and Burnside, following minor roads and farm tracks. The final short leg is on the B976 and B9158.

To link this route with the Firmounth Road (Walk 29), turn right after crossing Knockie Bridge and, at the next junction, turn left. Follow the track to Knockie Viewpoint where the Firmounth is joined.

Return route
Return to the start point by reversing the outward route. Alternatively follow Walk 29 in reverse from Braeloine Visitor Centre to Tarfside. Walk west on the road, crossing Water of Tarf, to join a signed track leading west to Invermark car park, 4.5km away.

Glen Tanar and Water of Tanar from the summit of Mount Keen

APPENDIX A
Walk summary table

Walk	Start	Finish (if linear)	Distance (km/miles)	Height gain (m/ft)	Time (hr/min)	Page
1 Monega Hill, Glas Maol, Creag Leacach and Monamenach	Auchavan, Glen Isla (NO 192 698)		21km (13 miles)	1242m (4075ft)	7hr	34
2 Badandun Hill	Freuchies, Glen Isla (NO 224 608)		22km (13¾ miles)	708m (2325ft)	6hr	40
3 Mount Blair	North of Altaltan on B951 (NO 182 638)		6km (3¾ miles)	500m (1640ft)	3hr	45
4 Mealna Letter	Angus/Perthshire boundary, 1km east of Cray on B951 (NO 153 642)		12.5km (7¾ miles)	475m (1560ft)	3hr 30min	49
5 Craigie Thieves	Backwater Reservoir dam, Glen Isla (NO 251 590)		25km (15½ miles)	786m (2580ft)	6hr 30min	54
6 Corwharn and Milldewan Hill	Backwater Reservoir, below Little Ley (NO 256 614)		15km (9¼ miles)	515m (1690ft)	4hr 15min	58
7 Craigie Law and Crock	Freuchies, Glen Isla (NO 224 608)		15km (9¼ miles)	440m (1445ft)	4hr	63

Walk	Start	Finish (if linear)	Distance (km/miles)	Height gain (m/ft)	Time (hr/min)	Page
8 Tulloch Hill, The Goal and Hill of Couternach	Tulloch Hill, 2km west of Dykehead (NO 371 606)		14km (8¾ miles)	500m (1640ft)	4hr	68
9 Cat Law and Long Goat	Turf Hill, 2km southeast of Easter Lednathie (NO 354 618)		11km (6¾ miles)	550m (1805ft)	3hr 30min	73
10 Knachly and Hill of Spott	Glenprosen Village (NO 328 657)		10km (6¼ miles)	340m (1115ft)	2hr 45min	77
11 Hill of Strone and Driesh	Glenprosen Lodge (NO 294 678)		20km (12½ miles)	930m (3050ft)	5hr 30min	81
12 Broad Cairn and Cairn Bannoch	Glen Doll Ranger Base (NO 283 761)		25km (15½ miles)	1000m (3280ft)	7hr	88
13 Tolmount and Tom Buidhe	Glen Doll Ranger Base (NO 283 761)		20km (12½ miles)	920m (3020ft)	6hr	93
14 Driesh and Mayar	Glen Doll Ranger Base (NO 283 761)		14km (8¾ miles)	900m (2955ft)	4hr 30min	98
15 Cairn Broadlands and Craig Mellon	Glen Doll Ranger Base (NO 283 761)		15km (9½ miles)	760m (2495ft)	5hr	103
16 Ferrowie and Lair of Aldararie	Glen Doll Ranger Base (NO 283 761)		13km (8 miles)	730m (2395ft)	4hr	107

183

Walk	Start	Finish (if linear)	Distance (km/miles)	Height gain (m/ft)	Time (hr/min)	Page
17 Ben Tirran	Adielinn Plantation on B955 (NO 352 715)		11km (63/4 miles)	730m (2395ft)	3hr 30min	111
18 Green Hill, Boustie Ley and Ben Reid	Clova (NO 326 730)		11.5km (71/4 miles)	800m (2625ft)	4hr	115
19 Dog Hillock, Finbracks and Manywe	Burn of Glenmoye (NO 402 646)		16km (10 miles)	680m (2230ft)	4hr 30min	119
20 Hill of Glansie	Glen Lethnot road, near Waterhead (NO 464 171)		13km (8 miles)	600m (1970ft)	4hr	124
21 Tamhilt and Hill of Mondurran	Glen Lethnot road 1.5km north of Craigendowie (NO 513 706)		16.5km (101/4 miles)	630m (2065ft)	4hr 30min	128
22 Hill of Wirren and East Wirren	Bridgend of Lethnot (NO 536 684)		14km (83/4 miles)	610m (2000ft)	4hr	132
23 Mount Battock and Mount Een	Millden Lodge (NO 540 789)		16km (10 miles)	730m (2395ft)	5hr	138
24 Hill of Cat and Hill of Gairney	Tarfside, Glen Esk (NO 492 797)		25km (151/2 miles)	1010m (3315ft)	7hr	143
25 Mount Keen	Invermark, Glen Esk (NO 447 803)		17km (101/2 miles)	720m (2360ft)	4hr 45min	148

Walk	Start	Finish (if linear)	Distance (km/miles)	Height gain (m/ft)	Time (hr/min)	Page
26 Craig Maskeldie and Hunt Hill	Invermark, Glen Esk (NO 447 803)		20km (12½ miles)	924m (3030ft)	6hr	152
27 Capel Mounth	Glen Doll Ranger Base (NO 283 761)	Spittal of Glenmuick, near Ballater (NO 307 850)	10km (6¼ miles)	540m (1770ft)	3hr	158
28 Tolmounth	Glen Doll Ranger Base (NO 283 761)	Auchallater, 3km south of Braemar (NO 155 882)	20km (12½ miles)	770m (2525ft)	6hr	163
29 Firmounth	Tarfside, Glen Esk (NO 492 797)	Braeloine Visitor Centre, Glen Tanar (NO 480 965)	18km (11¼ miles)	640m (2100ft)	5hr	169
30 Mounth	Invermark, Glen Esk (NO 447 803)	Braeloine Visitor Centre, Glen Tanar (NO 480 965)	23km (14¼ miles)	620m (2035ft)	6hr	175

APPENDIX B
Useful contacts

Estate information

The following is a list of estate contacts for walks where the route leads across land where deer stalking or game shooting takes place. Information for those marked HFTSH can be found online at www.outdooraccess-scotland.com/hftsh. When contacting an estate by telephone, please call at a reasonable hour. Where a website is listed, visit the 'contact' page for most up-to-date details. Details of stalking and shooting activities will often be found posted at access points and in car parks.

Walk 1	HFTSH	Walk 19	Hunthill Estate (email: gordon.kerr@smithsgore.co.uk)
Walk 2	Glen Isla Estate (tel: 01575 582227)	Walk 20	Glenogil Estate (www.glenogilestate.com)
Walk 4	HFTSH	Walk 21	Gannochy Estate (www.gannochyestate.co.uk)
Walk 5	No information available	Walk 22	Millden Estate (tel: 01356 670365): predominantly grouse shooting country, and no deer stalking on the estate.
Walk 6	No information available	Walk 23	HFTSH and Millden Estate (tel: 01356 670365)
Walk 9	Lednathie Estate (email: marshall@fiveacres.net)	Walk 24	HFTSH
Walk 10	Balnaboth Estate (www.glenprosen.co.uk)	Walk 25	HFTSH
Walk 11	Glenprosen Estate, c/o Savills (email: rwillis@savills.com)	Walk 27	HFTSH
Walk 12	HFTSH	Walk 28	HFTSH
Walk 14	HFTSH	Walk 29	HFTSH and Millden Estate (tel: 01356 670365)
Walk 16	Glenogil Estate (www.glenogilestate.com)	Walk 30	HFTSH

Area guides
Angus Glens
www.angusglens.co.uk
Information on the area, history, wildlife and people, plus links to accommodation.

Angus Ahead
www.angusahead.com
Tourism and leisure information plus events listings.

Paths and access
Angus Glens Ranger Service
The Ranger Base, Glen Doll DD8 4RD
Tel: 01575 550233
www.angus.gov.uk/leisure/rangerservice/angusglens.htm
Visitor information and guided walks.

Angus Glens Walking Festival
www.angusahead.com/walkingfestival
An annual four-day summer event.

Forestry Commission Scotland
www.forestry.gov.uk/scotland
Information on forest recreation.

Heading for the Scottish Hills
www.outdooraccess-scotland.com/hftsh
Stalking information (see Appendix B).

Heritage Paths
www.heritagepaths.co.uk
Database of historic routes through the mountains and glens.

Mountaineering Council of Scotland
www.mcofs.org.uk
Advice on all aspects of walking plus links to clubs and courses.

Outdoor Access Code
www.outdooraccess-scotland.com
Responsible access to the Scottish countryside.

Scottish Natural Heritage
www.snh.org.uk
Scottish Government's natural heritage agency.

Scottish Rights of Way and Access Society
www.scotways.com
Rights of way and access to the Scottish countryside.

Tayside Mountain Rescue
www.taysidemrt.org.uk
Mountain safety advice.

Public transport
Angus Council
www.angus.gov.uk/transport
Timetables for all public transport services in Angus.

Dundee Airport
www.hial.co.uk/dundee-airport

ScotRail
www.scotrail.co.uk

Scottish Citylink
www.citylink.co.uk

Stagecoach
www.stagecoachbus.com
Timetables for Stagecoach Strathtay bus services in Angus and Stagecoach Bluebird services in neighbouring Aberdeenshire.

Tourist information
Angus & Dundee Tourist Board
www.angusanddundee.co.uk

Visitor information and accommodation, with local tourist information centres at:

Brechin Museum
28 High Street, Brechin DD9 3ER
Tel: 01356 625536

Discovery Point
Discovery Quay
Dundee DD1 4XA
Tel: 01382 527527

Kirriemuir Gateway to the Glens Museum
32 High Street, Kirriemuir DD8 4BB
Tel: 01575 575479

Cairngorms National Park
www.visitcairngorms.co.uk
Visitor information and accommodation listings.

Outdoor Angus
www.outdoorangus.co.uk
Events listings and links to activity and accommodation providers.

Weather
Met Office
www.metoffice.gov.uk

Mountain Weather Information Service
www.mwis.org.uk

LISTING OF CICERONE GUIDES

The North-Western Fells
The Southern Fells
The Western Fells
Roads and Tracks of the Lake District
Rocky Rambler's Wild Walks
Scrambles in the Lake District North & South
Short Walks in Lakeland
1 South Lakeland
2 North Lakeland
3 West Lakeland
The Cumbria Coastal Way
The Cumbria Way and the Allerdale Ramble
Tour of the Lake District

DERBYSHIRE, PEAK DISTRICT AND MIDLANDS

High Peak Walks
Scrambles in the Dark Peak
The Star Family Walks
Walking in Derbyshire
White Peak Walks
The Northern Dales
The Southern Dales

SOUTHERN ENGLAND

A Walker's Guide to the Isle of Wight
Suffolk Coast & Heaths Walks
The Cotswold Way
The North Downs Way
The Peddars Way and Norfolk Coast Path
The Ridgeway National Trail
The South Downs Way
The South West Coast Path
The Thames Path
Walking in Berkshire
Walking in Kent
Walking in Sussex
Walking in the Isles of Scilly
Walking in the New Forest
Walking in the Thames Valley
Walking on Dartmoor
Walking on Guernsey
Walking on Jersey
Walking on the Isle of Wight
Walks in the South Downs National Park

WALES AND WELSH BORDERS

Backpacker's Britain – Wales

Glyndwr's Way
Great Mountain Days in Snowdonia
Hillwalking in Snowdonia
Hillwalking in Wales
Vols 1 & 2
Offa's Dyke Path
Ridges of Snowdonia
Scrambles in Snowdonia
The Ascent of Snowdon
Lleyn Peninsula Coastal Path
Pembrokeshire Coastal Path
The Shropshire Hills
The Wye Valley Walk
Walking in Pembrokeshire
Walking in the Forest of Dean
Walking in the South Wales Valleys
Walking on Gower
Walking on the Brecon Beacons
Welsh Winter Climbs

INTERNATIONAL CHALLENGES, COLLECTIONS AND ACTIVITIES

Canyoning
Europe's High Points
The Via Francigena (Canterbury to Rome): Part 1

EUROPEAN CYCLING

Cycle Touring in France
Cycle Touring in Ireland
Cycle Touring in Spain
Cycle Touring in Switzerland
Cycling in the French Alps
Cycling the Canal du Midi
Cycling the River Loire
The Danube Cycleway
The Grand Traverse of the Massif Central
The Rhine Cycle Route
The Way of St James

AFRICA

Climbing in the Moroccan Anti-Atlas
Kilimanjaro
Mountaineering in the Moroccan High Atlas
The High Atlas
Trekking in the Atlas Mountains
Walking in the Drakensberg

ALPS – CROSS-BORDER ROUTES

100 Hut Walks in the Alps
Across the Eastern Alps: E5
Alpine Points of View
Alpine Ski Mountaineering
1 Western Alps
2 Central and Eastern Alps
Chamonix to Zermatt
Snowshoeing
Tour of Mont Blanc
Tour of Monte Rosa
Tour of the Matterhorn
Trekking in the Alps
Walking in the Alps
Walks and Treks in the Maritime Alps

PYRENEES AND FRANCE/SPAIN CROSS-BORDER ROUTES

Rock Climbs in The Pyrenees
The GR10 Trail
The Mountains of Andorra
The Pyrenean Haute Route
The Pyrenees
The Way of St James France & Spain
Through the Spanish Pyrenees: GR11
Walks and Climbs in the Pyrenees

AUSTRIA

The Adlerweg
Trekking in Austria's Hohe Tauern
Trekking in the Stubai Alps
Trekking in the Zillertal Alps
Walking in Austria

EASTERN EUROPE

The High Tatras
The Mountains of Romania
Walking in Bulgaria's National Parks
Walking in Hungary

FRANCE

Chamonix Mountain Adventures
Ecrins National Park
GR20: Corsica
Mont Blanc Walks
Mountain Adventures in the Maurienne

The Cathar Way
The GR5 Trail
The Robert Louis Stevenson Trail
Tour of the Oisans: The GR54
Tour of the Queyras
Tour of the Vanoise
Trekking in the Vosges and Jura
Vanoise Ski Touring
Walking in the Auvergne
Walking in the Cathar Region
Walking in the Cevennes
Walking in the Dordogne
Walking in the Haute Savoie
  North & South
Walking in the Languedoc
Walking in the Tarentaise and
  Beaufortain Alps
Walking on Corsica

GERMANY

Germany's Romantic Road
Walking in the Bavarian Alps
Walking in the Harz Mountains
Walking the River Rhine Trail

HIMALAYA

Annapurna
Bhutan: A Trekker's Guide
Everest: A Trekker's Guide
Garhwal and Kumaon: A
  Trekker's and Visitor's Guide
Kangchenjunga: A Trekker's
  Guide
Langtang with Gosainkund and
  Helambu: A Trekker's Guide
Manaslu: A Trekker's Guide
The Mount Kailash Trek
Trekking in Ladakh

ICELAND & GREENLAND

Trekking in Greenland
Walking and Trekking in Iceland

IRELAND

Irish Coastal Walks
The Irish Coast to Coast Walk
The Mountains of Ireland

ITALY

Gran Paradiso
Sibillini National Park
Stelvio National Park
Shorter Walks in the Dolomites
Through the Italian Alps
Trekking in the Apennines

Trekking in the Dolomites
Via Ferratas of the Italian
  Dolomites: Vols 1 & 2
Walking in Abruzzo
Walking in Sardinia
Walking in Sicily
Walking in the Central Italian
  Alps
Walking in the Dolomites
Walking in Tuscany
Walking on the Amalfi Coast
Walking the Italian Lakes

MEDITERRANEAN

Jordan – Walks, Treks, Caves,
  Climbs and Canyons
The Ala Dag
The High Mountains of Crete
The Mountains of Greece
Treks and Climbs in Wadi Rum,
  Jordan
Walking in Malta
Western Crete

NORTH AMERICA

British Columbia
The Grand Canyon
The John Muir Trail
The Pacific Crest Trail

SOUTH AMERICA

Aconcagua and the Southern
  Andes
Hiking and Biking Peru's Inca
  Trails
Torres del Paine

SCANDINAVIA

Walking in Norway

SLOVENIA, CROATIA AND MONTENEGRO

The Julian Alps of Slovenia
The Mountains of Montenegro
Trekking in Slovenia
Walking in Croatia
Walking in Slovenia: The
  Karavanke

SPAIN AND PORTUGAL

Costa Blanca: West
Mountain Walking in Southern
  Catalunya
The Mountains of Central Spain
The Northern Caminos
Trekking through Mallorca

Walking in Madeira
Walking in Mallorca
Walking in the Algarve
Walking in the Cordillera
  Cantabrica
Walking in the Sierra Nevada
Walking on La Gomera and
  El Hierro
Walking on La Palma
Walking on Tenerife
Walking the GR7 in Andalucia
Walks and Climbs in the Picos
  de Europa

SWITZERLAND

Alpine Pass Route
Canyoning in the Alps
Central Switzerland
The Bernese Alps
The Swiss Alps
Tour of the Jungfrau Region
Walking in the Valais
Walking in Ticino
Walks in the Engadine

TECHNIQUES

Geocaching in the UK
Indoor Climbing
Lightweight Camping
Map and Compass
Mountain Weather
Outdoor Photography
Polar Exploration
Rock Climbing
Sport Climbing
The Book of the Bivvy
The Hillwalker's Guide to
  Mountaineering
The Hillwalker's Manual

MINI GUIDES

Avalanche!
Navigating with a GPS
Navigation
Pocket First Aid and Wilderness
  Medicine
Snow

For full information on all
our guides, and to order
books and eBooks, visit our
website:
www.cicerone.co.uk.

Walking – Trekking – Mountaineering – Climbing – Cycling

Over 40 years, Cicerone have built up an outstanding collection of 300 guides, inspiring all sorts of amazing adventures.

Every guide comes from extensive exploration and research by our expert authors, all with a passion for their subjects. They are frequently praised, endorsed and used by clubs, instructors and outdoor organisations.

All our titles can now be bought as **e-books** and many as iPad and Kindle files and we will continue to make all our guides available for these and many other devices.

Our website shows any **new information** we've received since a book was published. Please do let us know if you find anything has changed, so that we can pass on the latest details. On our **website** you'll also find some great ideas and lots of information, including sample chapters, contents lists, reviews, articles and a photo gallery.

It's easy to keep in touch with what's going on at Cicerone, by getting our monthly **free e-newsletter**, which is full of offers, competitions, up-to-date information and topical articles. You can subscribe on our home page and also follow us on **Facebook** and **Twitter**, as well as our **blog**.

Cicerone – the very best guides for exploring the world.

CICERONE

2 Police Square Milnthorpe Cumbria LA7 7PY
Tel: 015395 62069 info@cicerone.co.uk
www.cicerone.co.uk